20p

Discovering
FRENCH AND GERMAN
MILITARY UNIFORMS

Arthur Taylor

D1612640

Illustrations by the author

Shire Publications Ltd.

CONTENTS

INTRODUCTION

This book is intended as a companion to *Discovering British Military Uniforms* in that its primary purpose is to bring together in reference form scattered information on uniform details. It is hoped that this will prove of service to military modellers, wargamers and others interested in the dress of soldiers, and save them from the necessity of hunting through a number of sources before they can begin operations.

It has the further object, however, of explaining the background to the development of the uniforms of the two most important armies in Europe's history. Items of military dress are not a matter of caprice; behind them usually lies a wealth of history, written in terms of human courage and suffering on the level of the soldier in the ranks, and pride and ambition, often not well-intentioned, on the level of his leaders. Thus the story of an army's uniforms is the story of the army itself and the nation behind it, and therefore interesting in its own right.

The book might well bear the sub-title 'From Napoleon to Hitler'. To cover the same time-span as *Discovering British Military Uniforms* for the armies of both France and Germany would not be possible in a book of this size. The Napoleonic War, therefore, is the obvious starting point since it is a watershed in both the history of warfare and the history of military fashions. In the case of the latter, distinct national styles of uniform are a characteristic of the nineteenth century. Other ages found war romantic, the later middle ages for example, with the code of chivalry to hide the unpleasant nature of violent death. In those days, however, war was the pastime and duty of warrior aristocrats, individualists all, for whom personal heraldry was more important than uniformity.

In the nineteenth century war was equally romanticised, but this time by European liberals and idealists. It had also become a mass pursuit involving large conscript armies, hence uniforms. In both instances, however, colour and style of dress were intended to convey something of the national philosophy behind the business of battle.

The period chosen opens with the French dominating Europe under the leadership of a Corsican tyrant; it closes with the Germans holding the lordship, inspired by an Austrian dictator. Between the two sets of circumstances lay one of the most titanic struggles in military history, with the German and French armies as the main contestants.

Who won in the end? Is Berlin or Paris the capital of Europe? This issue still awaits a decision. The Prussian military theorist, Clausewitz, wrote that war is 'diplomacy carried on by other means'. It is, however, not the only means of achieving what he considered to be the aim of war-making—'to compel our opponent to fulfil our will'.

THE FRENCH ARMY

The French army was involved in practically all the major wars of the eighteenth century, and without doubt was the most professional of the European armies, setting the pace for all the others in organisational and theoretical matters. Its artillery, moulded by such minds as General de Gribeauval (1715-89) and General de Teil (1738-1820), was outstanding in its technical competence, and it was in this branch of the service that the young Napoleon received his military education. The year after he began his service, his regiment was the demonstration unit at the School of Artillery under de Teil himself. Indeed, all that the French army lacked at this time was great commanders.

This expertise was transmitted to the armies of the Revolution, despite the political confusion of the times, which served to clear some of the dead wood from the upper commissioned ranks and permit the rise of more dynamic personalities from below. The Household Troops were abolished as a matter of principle, and royal or territorial titles of regiments were replaced by numbers as part of the general levelling taking place throughout French society. Nevertheless, it was basically with the old Royal Army that the ideologues proceeded to make profitable war on the rest of Europe, suitably cloaked under egalitarian propaganda which disguised inherited national ambitions.

The result was that at the beginning of the nineteenth century the continent of Europe lay prostrate before French military might, while at home Frenchmen lived quite happily for the most part under a show of efficiency provided by military dictatorship.

In 1804 Napoleon marked the new order in Europe by establishing France as an empire, with himself as hereditary emperor.

The First Empire, 1804-14

During the republican years, a Guard unit had existed which by 1802 had grown into the Consular Guard of two Grenadier battalions, two of Chasseurs, a regiment of Horse Grenadiers, another of Chasseurs à Cheval, and artillery. These now became the senior regiments of the Imperial Guard, almost ten thousand strong, and Napoleon added more units to this elite formation as time passed, until it numbered over 126,000 in 1815. The principal components were as follows:

Title	Raised	Uniform	Remarks
CORPS OF GRENADIERS A PIED			
Grenadiers à pied	1804	See F1.	Old Guard. A 2nd Regiment existed 1806-8, another raised 1811. See below for Grenadiers Hollandais
Fusiliers Grenadiers	1806	See F2.	Middle Guard
Tirailleurs Grenadiers	1809	See F3. Gaiters as F25.	Young Guard. Five additional regiments subsequently
Conscrit Grenadiers	1809	Shako as F3. Coat as F3 O.R.s but with collar and cuffs as F1; white turnbacks; shoulder-straps and gaiters as F25.	Young Guard
Flanqueurs Grenadiers	1811	Shako as F2, red cords, red over yellow pompon. Coat as F25 but all-green piped yellow with F3-styled cuff piping; red turnbacks with white eagle badges. Yellow tassels on black gaiters.	Young Guard. Originally recruited from foresters
CORPS OF CHASSEURS A PIED			
Chasseurs à pied	1804	Bearskin as for F1 without plate; plume, red over green. F1 coat, but cuffs as F3; green epaulettes with red horn badges on turnbacks (F27). F1 gaiters but black.	Old Guard. 2nd regiment raised 1806
Fusiliers-Chasseurs	1806	Shako as F2; plume, red over green. Remainder as for Chasseurs à pied.	Middle Guard
Tirailleurs-Chasseurs	1809	Shako as F2 without side lace; green pompon. Coat as for Chasseurs, but red collar, blue lapels piped white, F25 shoulder-straps green piped red, turnbacks red piped white with green eagle badges. F25 gaiters.	Young Guard
Conscrit-Chasseurs	1809	Shako as F2, with green tuft. Coat as F3, but lapels blue piped white, collar red piped white, F25 shoulder-straps blue piped white, turnbacks blue piped red with green horn badges. White waistcoat; blue trousers over black gaiters as F33.	Young Guard. Two regiments

Title	Raised	Uniform	Remarks
Flanqueurs-Chasseurs	1813	As for Flanqueurs-Grenadiers but white shako cords, yellow over green tuft, red cuffs, green horn badges on turnbacks, green tassels on gaiters.	Young Guard
CAVALRY			
Grenadiers à Cheval	1804	See F10.	
Chasseurs à Cheval	1804	See F11, F12, F13.	
Dragoons (Empress's)	1806	Helmet, F9. Remainder as for F10, but coat green.	
LIGHT HORSE LANCERS			
1st (Polish) Regiment	1807	See F8.	3rd (Polish) Regiment raised 1812, but survivors of Moscow campaign incorporated in 1st. Dressed as 1st but yellow lace, etc.
2nd (Dutch) Regiment	1810	As F8 but scarlet cap top, jacket, trousers; blue collar, lapels, stripes; yellow lace; brass buttons; pennon white over red.	

F1 Foot Grenadiers of the Guard, 1812.
Grenadier in full dress. Cap: black bearskin; white cords; brass plate; red plume with national tricolour cockade at base; red crown with white grenade badge (F6). Coat: blue; white lapels and cuff flap; red epaulettes, cuffs and turnbacks and piping on tails (F4); brass buttons and grenade badges on tails. White waistcoat, breeches, gaiters, and equipment straps. Blue greatcoat roll; hide-covered pack; black pouch with brass ornaments as in F7.

F2 Fusilier-Grenadiers of the Guard, 1812.
Grenadier in full dress. Shako: black; white cords and chevron lace; brass fittings; red plume, national cockade at base. Remainder of uniform as for F1, except for white epaulettes with two red central lines.

F3 Sharpshooter-Grenadiers of the Guard, 1810
Officer. Shako: as for F2 with gilt fittings and cords. Coat: blue; gilt epaulettes, buttons, gorget; red cuffs and turnbacks piped white; tail piping in white (ORs had red shoulder-straps piped white; red collar and shako-hangings; blue lapels). White waistcoat, belt, breeches, gloves. Black boots turned down.

F4 Piping on coat-tails, Foot Grenadiers of the Guard.

F5 Imperial Eagle shako badge.

F6 White grenade badge on cap of Foot Grenadiers of the Guard.

F7 Pouch of Foot Grenadiers of the Guard.

F
4
5
6
2
1
3
7

7

Scouts	1813		
Title	Raised	Uniform	Remarks
1st Regiment		Old Guard section: Shako as F18 with red pompon and lace band around top. Green hussar uniform (F12, F13, F17) with white lace buttons; red collar, cuffs on jacket and stripe on trousers; red and white sash; black fur trim. Young Guard section: as above but plain green jacket piped red on top and front of collar, front and bottom edge of jacket, shoulder-strap edges	Attached to Horse Grenadiers

F8 Light Horse Lancers of the Guard, 1812.
Lancer of the 1st (Polish) Regiment. Cap: black leather; brass plate; crimson top; white plume and hangings; white metal fittings. Jacket: blue; crimson lapels edged white; white epaulettes and aiguillette, white metal buttons. Crimson trousers, blue stripes. White gauntlets, and belts; brass buckles; black leather pouch on shoulder-belt with eagle badge. Black boots. Brass scabbard. (Lance pennon, red over white.)

F9 Helmet of the Guard Dragoons, 1812.
Other ranks' helmet. Brass, black mane and tuft, panther-skin turban. Red plume on left in parade dress.

F10 Horse Grenadiers of the Guard, 1812.
Grenadier. As for F1 with these exceptions: cap hangings, epaulettes and aiguillette light orange (aurore); no cap plate; white gauntlets; brass scabbard.

F11 Chasseurs à Cheval of the Guard, 1812.
Chasseur in dismounted service dress. Cap: black fur; scarlet bag lines and tasselled yellow; yellow hangings; red over green plume; national cockade with brass eagle in centre; brass chinscales. Coat: green; scarlet collar, cuffs, lapel piping; yellow piping on cuffs, epaulettes and aiguillette; horn badges on turnbacks; brass buttons. Scarlet waistcoat laced yellow, brass buttons. Green breeches, yellow lace knots and stripe down outside seams. White belts, shoulder pouch as F8. Black boots with yellow trim and tassels. Brass scabbard.

F12 Mounted full dress.
Green jacket with scarlet cuff.

F13 Scarlet pelisse with black fur.
Yellow lace, brass buttons. Yellow doeskin breeches.

F

8

9

10

11

12

13

Title	Raised	Uniform	Remarks
		(F25 style), edge of tails, top of cuff (F11 style). No lapels or pelisse.	
2nd Regiment		Cap as F20, crimson; orange lines; green pompon; national cockade on centre front held by yellow button lace. Remainder, as for Young Guard section of 1st, with crimson piping, collar, cuffs and turnbacks.	Attached to Dragoons
3rd Regiment		As for 1st Lancers, but for grey-buttoned overalls.	Attached to 1st Lancers

There were other miscellaneous units, such as the squadron of Mamelouks attached to the Chasseurs, a souvenir of Napoleon's Egyptian campaign dressed in Arab style. The Grenadiers Hollandais were incorporated in the Guard in 1810, when Holland was united to France. Their uniform was exactly the same as F1, but without the cap plate and with a white coat with crimson collars, cuffs, lapels, turnbacks and rear piping. The Guard Horse Artillery dressed as Hussars (F11, but all-red plume; white bag piping; blue coat, waistcoat, breeches; red lace, piping and tassels; white buttons. Blue F12 and F13 in full dress, with red lace, white buttons. Jacket had red cuffs, pelisse black fur trim). For the Foot Artillery, see F14.

The two senior regiments of the line cavalry were the Carabiniers (see F16), which had preserved their identity and status from the Royal Army, and until 1810 wore the blue coat of the old royal heavy cavalry in a uniform not unlike F10 with red lapels and the yellow belt. By a decision of the previous year they were re-equipped as Cuirassiers and given the uniform illustrated.

Of the old heavy cavalry regiments, the 8th were the original wearers of the cuirass with the title Cuirassiers du Roi. In 1803, the heavy cavalry regiments were reduced to twelve, all of which were armed as Cuirassiers (F15). The uniform dates from 1802, and the regimental distinctives were:

1st, 2nd, 3rd Regiments: scarlet (2nd—blue cuff, flap piped scarlet; 3rd—blue cuff, flap and cuff piping scarlet).

4th, 5th, 6th Regiments: orange (aurore) (5th—blue cuff, flap piped aurore; 6th—blue cuff, flap and cuff piping aurore).

7th, 8th, 9th Regiments: primrose (8th—blue cuff, flap piped primrose; 9th—blue cuff, flap and cuff piping primrose).

10th, 11th, 12th Regiments: pink (11th—blue cuff, flap piped pink; 12th—blue cuff, flap and cuff piping pink).

The distinguishing marks of the Dragoons were green coats and brass helmets, features which dated from 1763. The eighteen Royal Army regiments were numbered in 1791 and assumed the regimental facing colours which continued into the Empire, during which time their total was increased to thirty. The brass helmet was similar to F15 with a brown turban; the green jacket was like F19, with tail decorations as for F4 (except that in some regiments the pocket flaps were arranged horizontally). Buff breeches, white belts and gauntlets, and jacked boots completed the uniform.

In the following table, the regimental colour was worn on collar, lapels, cuffs, cuff flaps, turnbacks and rear pocket piping by the first regiment in each group only. The second regiment in each had green collars and cuff flaps, and the third regiment in each, green cuffs.

1st, 2nd, 3rd Regiments: scarlet, horizontal rear pockets.
4th, 5th, 6th Regiments: scarlet, vertical pockets.
7th, 8th, 9th Regiments: crimson, horizontal pockets.
10th, 11th, 12th Regiments: crimson, vertical pockets.
13th, 14th, 15th Regiments: pink, horizontal pockets.
16th, 17th, 18th Regiments: pink, vertical pockets.
19th, 20th, 21st Regiments: primrose, horizontal pockets.
22nd, 23rd, 24th Regiments: primrose, vertical pockets.
25th, 26th, 27th Regiments: aurore, horizontal pockets.
28th, 29th, 30th Regiments: aurore, vertical pockets.

In 1811 1st, 3rd, 8th, 9th, 10th and 29th Dragoons were converted to Lancers and were not replaced in the numbered list, which thereafter had gaps in it. The new Light Horse Lancers wore a modification of their former dragoon uniform (F19), but three additional Lancer regiments of Polish and German origin wore the Polish uniform (F8). The regimental colours of the French regiments were:

1st Regiment: scarlet   4th Regiment: crimson
2nd Regiment: aurore   5th Regiment: sky-blue
3rd Regiment: pink   6th Regiment: cherry-red

The normal type of light cavalry were the Chasseurs à Cheval, of which there were twelve regiments in the old army, being increased to thirty-one by 1812. Up to 1804-6 they wore a green hussar jacket with white piping (F12) with a tapered felt cap, changing at various times to a green coat piped in white in the style of F11 and shako (F17) with white cords and green plume tipped with the regimental colour. Breeches were as F18. The 4th, 5th, 6th and 10th Regiments retained the hussar jacket. In 1806 the regimental colours were as follows, with the second regiment in each group of three having a green collar, the third

green cuffs, instead of the appropriate colour:
1st, 2nd, 3rd Regiments: scarlet
4th, 5th, 6th Regiments: primrose
7th, 8th, 9th Regiments: pink
10th, 11th, 12th Regiments: crimson
13th, 14th, 15th Regiments: true orange
16th Regiment: sky-blue
(17th and 18th disbanded)
19th, 20th, 21st Regiments: aurore
22nd, 23rd, 24th Regiments: nasturtium (but 24th had primrose
  collar and nasturtium cuffs)
25th, 26th Regiments madder-red

At this stage elite companies wore a fur cap (F11) with a plume and bag of the regimental colour, the plume being at the front instead of the side, and red epaulettes. In 1812 the uniform was standardised as F18. The regimental distinctives of regiments additional to or otherwise than the above tables were:
17th and 18th Regiments had been revived, with appropriate

F14   **Foot Artillery of the Guard, 1812.**
Gunner. Shako: black; red plume, pompon, lace band on top rim, hangings; national cockade; brass eagle, chin-strap. Coat: blue; red piping, epaulettes, cuffs; tail piping as F4, with red turnbacks and blue grenade badges; brass buttons. Blue waistcoat and breeches. White belts and gaiters. Black leather pouch with eagle badge surmounting two crossed cannon. Cutlass as F2. (Unit also wore bearskin cap as F1, without plate but with leather peak; hangings red; grenade badge on crown yellow.)

F15   **Cuirassiers, 1812.**
Trooper. Helmet: white metal, brass comb and fittings, black leather peak, black mane, tuft, turban, red plume. Coat: blue, red epaulettes; collar, cuffs, cuff button flaps, turnbacks and tail piping in regimental colours (see text); collar piping blue; white metal buttons, grenade ornaments. Steel cuirass, red lining edged white. Buff breeches. White belts and gauntlets. Black leather boots and cartridge pouch.

F16   **Carabiniers, 1810.**
Trooper. Helmet: brass; white metal fittings; red crest. Coat: white; sky-blue collar piped white; sky-blue cuff flaps, turnbacks, rear piping (F15); white metal buttons and grenade ornaments; red epaulettes; 1st Regiment—red cuffs, 2nd—sky-blue. Cuirass: brass-covered steel; blue lining edged white. Yellow shoulder-belt edged white. White breeches, gauntlets. Rest as F15.

14

15

16

differences in the sky-blue group.

23rd Regiment had both collar and cuffs nasturtium.

24th Regiment had the correct nasturtium collar and green cuffs.

27th Regiment, madder-red with green cuffs.

28th, 29th, 30th Regiments, purple.

31st Regiment, buff, with a lance-cap head-dress.

Hussars were the most extravagantly dressed cavalrymen in any army at this time. The Royal Army had six regiments of them, one of which, the Hussars of Conflans, remained true to the monarchy and crossed to the anti-revolutionary side. The republicans made up the number from two volunteer regiments with the propaganda titles Liberty and Equality, and by 1810 the number had risen to ten. The Hungarian fashion was the

F17   1st Hussars, 1807.

Hussar. Shako: black, white hangings; badge and cockade as F18; black plume; pompon of company colour. Jacket: sky-blue; scarlet cuffs; white lace; white metal buttons. Breeches: sky-blue; white stripe on side seams and rump; knot on thighs similar to F11. White belts; brass buckles; black pouch. Brass scabbard. Black sabretache with scarlet front edged white. Black boots, white tops and tassels.

F18   Chasseurs à Cheval, 1812.

Chasseur. Shako: black; national cockade; white metal badge and chinscales; pompon of regimental colour (see text). Coatee: green; collar, cuffs, turnbacks, piping of regimental colour; rear decoration F21, with green horn badges; white metal buttons. Green breeches; white stripes and thigh loops. Boots, belts as F17. White-metal scabbard.

F19   Light Horse Lancers, 1812.

Trooper. Helmet: brass; brown turban; black leather peak; black fur crest. Coatee: green; collar, cuffs (F18 style), lapels, turnbacks, piping of regimental colour (see text); rear decoration F21, with green eagle badges on turnbacks; brass buttons. Overalls: green; wide stripe of regimental colour with brass buttons on outside seams, reinforced with black leather inside and bottom of legs for breeches and boots as F18, with yellow instead of white). White gauntlets. Belts and scabbard as F18. Pennon, red over white.

F20   Later type of Hussar shako.

Red; black peak and rear flap, hangings; national cockade; Chasseurs à Cheval plume if worn.

F21   Coatee, rear decoration (see F18, F19).

F

17

18

19

20

21

15

hallmark of the Hussar's uniform (see F11, F12, F13, F17) but only the elite companies wore the fur cap, with a red plume and bag. In 1812 the grenadier shako was ordered for them, with the red plume (F26). Of the remainder, some wore the normal shako (F18) with an eagle or lozenge badge, and some the cylindrical shako (F20). Regimental differences in 1812 were:

	Jacket	Collar	Cuffs	Lace	Pelisse	Breeches	Buttons
1st	sky-blue		red	white		green	white
2nd	red-brown		sky-blue	white		sky-blue	white
3rd	silver-grey		red	red			white
4th	imperial blue		scarlet	yellow	scarlet		yellow
5th	sky-blue		white	lemon	white		yellow
6th	scarlet		scarlet	yellow	imperial blue	imperial blue	yellow
7th	dark green	scarlet	scarlet	yellow		scarlet	yellow
8th	dark green	scarlet	scarlet	white		scarlet	white
9th	scarlet	sky-blue	sky-blue	yellow	sky-blue	mid-blue	yellow
10th	sky-blue	scarlet	scarlet	white			white
11th	imperial blue	scarlet	scarlet	yellow			yellow

(Where there is no entry, the colour is the same as the jacket. The second colour of the crimson-striped girdle is the same as the button colour.)

The infantry regiments of the Royal Army wore a uniform similar to F22, with the traditional Bourbon white instead of blue. Grenadiers wore bearskin caps. The alleged democratisa-

F22　Infantryman, 1793-1804.
Black hat, pouch, gaiters and boots. White waistcoat, breeches, belts. Coat: blue, lined white; white lapels and cuff button flap; red collar, cuffs, epaulettes; red piping on edge of lapels, cuff flap, coat fronts and skirts; white piping on edge of collar, and on cuffs; brass buttons.

F23　Light Infantry shako badge plate, 1810.
White metal.

F24　Infantry shako badge plate, 1810.
Brass.

F25　Infantryman, 1812.
Fusilier shako: black; brass fittings with badge as F26; national cockade; pompon of company colour (see text). Coatee: blue; white lapels, lining, turnbacks; red collar and cuffs piped white; blue shoulder-straps and cuff flaps piped red; red piping on lapels and rear pocket flaps (see F4); cypher badge on turnbacks, blue (see F27), brass buttons. White breeches; black gaiters and boots. White belts. Grey greatcoat roll; hide pack, plain black pouch.

F26　Infantry shako, flank companies, 1812.
Black, brass plate and fittings. Chevrons, tuft, top and bottom rim lace, red for Grenadiers, yellow for Volti-geurs; national cockade.

F

22

23

24

25

26

tion of the army was marked by the assumption of the blue, red and white (the original order from the centre outwards) national cockade, and the substitution of the blue of the National Guard (the instrument of the politicians) for white as the coat colour. In 1804 the standardisation of infantry dress was set on foot, although it was never completely successful. By now the grenadier cap had been largely abandoned, and shakos began to replace the cocked hats. For a while an attempt was made to restore the Bourbon white perhaps as an indication of Napoleon's view of his status, but it did not succeed. The shako had a lozenge-shaped plate (F24), white hangings, the cockade, and pompon of the company colour when worn by centre companies (1st—green, 2nd—blue, 3rd—orange, 4th—violet). Grenadier shakos had red plumes and embellishments, Voltigeurs' yellow. Likewise, the shoulder-straps of centre companies were blue piped red (F25 style), Grenadiers had red epaulettes, Voltigeurs had yellow collars and cuffs and green and yellow epaulettes.

In 1812 a new-pattern uniform was decreed (F25, F26, F27). Grenadiers now had scarlet shoulder-straps piped blue, and Voltigeurs had buff collars and shoulder-straps piped blue. They wore scarlet grenade- and buff horn-badges on their turnbacks, as appropriate.

Light Infantry regiments wore an all-blue uniform (F28), with white piping and scarlet collars, being the first to adopt the shako. When the pre-1812 coat was worn, there were some occa-

F27   Infantry turnback badges.
See text.
F28   Light Infantry, 1812.
Junior officer. Shako: black; silver lace and fittings; green pompon. Coatee: blue; scarlet collar; silver epaulettes; silver buttons; white piping. Blue breeches. Black boots topped and tasselled with silver. White belt. Gilt gorget.
F29   3rd Swiss Regiment, 1809.
Voltigeur. Shako: black; black chinstrap; brass badge, white hangings; French national cockade; green over yellow plume. Coat: red; black lapels and cuffs; red cuff flaps; yellow collar; green epaulettes; white piping and turnbacks; brass buttons. White belts, waistcoat, breeches. Black gaiters. (Other companies, black collars. Grenadiers —white epaulettes, bearskin caps: scarlet plume, national cockade, white hangings, brass plate and chinscales. Centre companies—red shoulder-strap piped white; shako: as above with company colour pompon.)
F30   Musket, 1801 pattern.

F

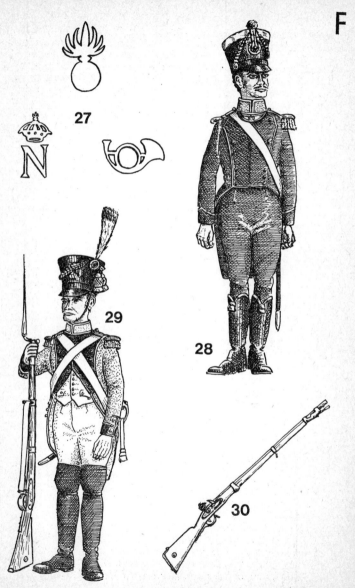

27

29

28

30

sional variations—green epaulettes, red lapels, cuffs or cuff flaps—depending on the regiment. A green plume might be worn on the side of the shako (F29) or centre, or a green pompon, with the normal white hangings, cockade and badge plate (F23). The equivalent of the Grenadiers, the Carabiniers, wore bearskin caps with red plumes, white hangings and no plate, together with red epaulettes, while Voltigeurs had yellow shako distinctives, green and yellow epaulettes and yellow collars. A unique feature of the Light Infantry was its leg-wear, short black gaiters topped and tasselled with green, red or yellow as appropriate. The adoption of the 1812 coatee ironed out many of the regimental differences, centre companies in particular having the standard shoulder-strap, piped white. The turnback badges of Carabinier companies carried grenade badges, centre companies and Voltigeurs having horns.

The Foot Artillery, before the 1812 regulations, wore a uniform identical to F14, except that the shako had an additional band of red lace around the bottom, a smaller plume and lozenge badge. The shoulder straps were as for F25, and the pouch had crossed cannons only. Subsequently, the uniform was as for F25, with a blue collar piped red, blue lapels and breeches, turnbacks as F14, the two-belt equipment, and a shako like the grenadier version of F26. Horse Artillery changed from a version of F17 (all-blue jacket and breeches; red lace and pipings; red and blue girdle; red shako embellishments; crossed cannons on pouch) to one of F18 (blue jacket and breeches; red lace and pipings *but* blue cuff piped red; red epaulettes, collar and shako as for Foot Artillery).

F31 Royal Guard Infantry, 1815.
> *Grenadier. Bearskin cap: brass plate; white hangings. Coat: blue; red lining, cuffs, epaulettes; white lace; white metal buttons. White belts and breeches. Black gaiters and boots.*

F32 Horse Grenadiers of the Royal Guard, 1816.
> *Senior NCO. Bearskin cap: white hangings; brass chinscales; yellow-over-red plume. Coat: blue, piped red; white lace and epaulettes; white metal buttons; white grenade badges. White belts, breeches, gauntlets. Black boots.*

F33 Line Light Infantry, 1822.
> *Grenadier. Shako: black; brass badge and chinscales; yellow lace band; red plume. Coatee: blue; yellow collar, piping; red epaulettes; brass buttons. White trousers (blue in winter) and spats. White belts; hide pack, etc.*

F

31

32

33

The Bourbon Restoration, 1815-30

The French army lived on after the defeat of its greatest commander, purged of Napoleonic symbols, subjected to a formal disbandment and recreation in the name of Louis XVIII, and deprived of only the most irreconcilable of its professional elements—few in practice.

A Royal Guard was established, of eight infantry regiments (two of which were Swiss wearing red instead of blue coatees), horse and foot artillery, and eight cavalry regiments. Of these, two were Cuirassiers, new to the Guard and wearing a uniform not unlike F15 with a crested helmet like F16. There were two regiments of Horse Grenadiers (F32), one of Dragoons (crested brass helmet; green coatee, rose-pink lapels), one of Lancers (as F8, green jacket and trousers; crimson cap and plastron; white embellishments and trouser stripes), and one of Hussars (fur cap, white plume, red bag; blue jacket, red collar and cuffs; blue pelisse, black fur; crimson breeches, white lace).

The line cavalry consisted of a regiment of Carabiniers (still uniformed as F16), six of Cuirassiers, ten of Dragoons, twenty-four of Chasseurs à Cheval, and six of Hussars. (Jackets and pelisses: 1st—sky-blue, 2nd—maroon, 3rd—light grey, 4th—red, 5th—dark blue, 6th—green. Red trousers with two stripes of the jacket colour for all but 4th—sky-blue; red shakos for all but 4th—black; red collars for all but 4th—blue; black pelisses, fur trim, sabretaches.)

The line infantry originally wore a white version of F25 with coloured lapels and a shako more like F33. The centre companies' turnbacks now bore the Bourbon fleur-de-lys. In 1820 they received a new uniform, F33, which was worn by all infantry, the ordinary infantry having the F25 style cuff. After an initial attempt to establish different regimental facings, all ordinary infantry wore a red collar, Light Infantry a yellow collar. Grenadier companies wore red fringed epaulettes, Voltigeurs yellow.

During the 1820s the French army was again campaigning abroad in Spain and Greece, in pursuance of objects which enjoyed the blessing of the small coterie of international statesmen by whose efforts the stability of Europe was carefully rebuilt and maintained after the long war of the demagogues of the Enlightenment. All was well again, and by the end of the reign the army had opened up its long association with Algeria with which its fortunes and honour were linked until the second half of the twentieth century. Then came the Revolution of 1830, and a new monarch.

The reign of Louis Phillippe, 1830-48

It was during the dull, middle-class dominated reign of the 'Citizen-King' that Napoleon's statue was re-erected in the Place Vendôme, the Arc de Triomphe was raised in honour of his victories, and finally, in 1840, the great Emperor's ashes were brought home from St Helena to a place of honour in the Invalides. Notwithstanding all this nostalgia, the reign stamped its own styles upon the uniforms of the army which were to persist through further political upheavals and be accepted (and emulated) in military circles the world over as 'typically French'.

The Royal Guards were abolished at the outset of the reign, of course, as a political gesture. The Lancers were taken into the line cavalry and designated, from the king's family name, the Lanciers d'Orleans—perhaps the nearest thing to House-hold Troops which the circumstances of the reign would allow. They wore their former uniform and, when five regiments of Chasseurs à Cheval were converted to Lancers in 1831 (F38), took precedence after them. The fourteen Chasseur regiments wore the uniform F37 from 1831, except that the fur cap did not succeed the shako (black, with black weeping plume) until the mid-forties. In addition, there were six Hussar regiments, ten Cuirassiers, and the two regiments of Carabiniers. The latter had been reformed in 1825, but they now lost their white coatees (F36). There were twelve regiments of Dragoons (F35).

A new feature of the army, marking the blossoming of the French colonial empire, was the creation in Algeria in 1830 (some authorities say 1831) of the Chasseurs d'Afrique. Origin-ally dressed in Polish style, the lance and lance cap were not much in evidence after 1833 although still the regulation. The rakish *casquette d'Afrique* was preferred in the corps, and the baggy red breeches with false leather boots attached made their first appearance among them (F39). As a counterpart in 1834 three regiments of native light horse were raised, the Spahis, officered chiefly but not exclusively by Frenchmen, and wearing a uniform based upon Arab dress.

1831 also saw the creation of the Foreign Legion, foreign mercenaries to be recruited for service outside France. This continued a long and honourable tradition of the French service which stretched back to 1494 when Charles VIII of France launched the era of modern wars by invading Italy with an army which included Swiss and German pikemen. Closer in time were the Scottish and Irish regiments of the eighteenth-century Royal Army, and above all others, the red-coated Swiss Guards. By an 1803 Treaty of Alliance Switzerland supplied four regiments to Napoleon's army in its turn (only eighty survivors of the 3rd Regiment came back from the Moscow campaign), and the presence of Swiss regiments in the Restoration Guard has been noted. Former members of these now enlisted in the new Legion, providing the backbone of what came to be the 1st Battalion of the seven. The 2nd and 3rd Battalions were formed from Swiss and German recruits, and the organisation and training of what looked initially an unpromising rabble was in the hands of a Swiss, Colonel Stoffel. Within a year he had produced an efficient fighting force, the first of whose members to be in action were companies of the 3rd Battalion.

This first Legion had a short life. In 1835, after successful work in Algeria, to honour a treaty obligation, it was ceded to the Spanish government, then involved in civil war. Two and a half years later, when it was disbanded in Spain, only five hundred of the original five thousand remained. Four hundred of the survivors chose to return to Algeria to join the Second Legion, raised in 1835 after the departure of the First, and which has had a continuous existence ever since.

From Algeria spread styles of dress which were to influence fashions of the rest of the infantry. The red trousers were adopted in 1829, so that the standard was as F34. On campaign, however, the shako yielded to the red cloth *casquette d'Afrique* with its leather peak. The trousers were tucked into the gaiters, the greatcoat was worn with its skirts buttoned back, the coatee was stowed away for parade use and the white crossbelts were laid aside. The 1845 regulations embodied the fruits

F34   Line Infantry, 1833.
      Grenadier. Shako: black; red lace and double pompon; brass fittings. Coatee: blue; red collar, epaulettes; cuffs and piping, brass buttons. Red trousers, white spats, black boots. White belts. Grey greatcoat roll, hide pack, black pouch.

F35   3rd Dragoons, 1838.
      Dragoon. Helmet: brass; black 'brush' and tuft; red plume, green base. Coatee: dark green; red epaulettes; rose-pink plastron, cuffs and piping, brass buttons. White belts, black pouch. White gloves. Red trousers, black boots.

F36   1st Carabiniers, 1845.
      Trooper. Helmet: brass; red crest. Coatee: light blue; red collar, epaulettes. Cuirass: steel, coated with brass; brass fittings, breast decoration brass centre with white metal surround; red lining; black leather belt. White belt and gauntlets. Red trousers, black boots.

F

35

36

34

of this experience. A new shako modelled on the *casquette* (F40, F41) was authorised, and black leather equipment. A full-skirted tunic (as F41) was normal wear, but the campaigning dress was as in F42. It is instructive to compare this with the later illustrations, F53, F59 and F63.

Another new corps raised in this reign was one of riflemen, the Chasseurs d'Orleans, created in 1838 as the Tirailleurs de Vincennes and retaining that title until 1842. After the revolution of 1848 which deposed the Orleanist monarch, they became the Chasseurs à Pied. They were quite distinct from the twenty-five regiments of Light Infantry, and wore a distinctive uniform (see F41).

During these years the artillery at least had remained free from change of radical nature. The Restoration Royal Corps of Artillery had consisted of eight regiments of foot artillery and four of horse. The two branches had been amalgamated in 1829, with identical uniforms other than practical differences dictated by mounted service. There were ten regiments altogether (see F40).

The army stood apart from politics. It moved neither to defend Louis Philippe nor to throw him out. On behalf of the new republic, the soldiers of General Cavaignac ruthlessly suppressed a rising of Parisian workers led by extremists in the 'June days' of 1848. In the following year, they besieged Rome at the behest of the elected President of France, Louis Napoleon, nephew of the Emperor. The revolutionary republicans of Garibaldi were ejected, and a French garrison was installed to safeguard it for the Pope. It seemed that the day

F37   6th Chasseurs à Cheval, 1843.
      Trooper, first class. Cap: black fur; black plume, red boss; black leather chinstrap. Jacket: dark green; yellow cuffs, lace, collar patch; white epaulettes and cap lines; white metal buttons. White belts and gloves. Red trousers reinforced with black leather. Black boots.

F38   Lancers, 1853.
      Lancer. Cap: black; blue top; brass fittings; yellow piping; red plume. Jacket: blue, with yellow lapels, collar, cuffs; white epaulettes; brass buttons. White cap lines, belts, gloves. Red trousers with double blue stripe. Black boots and pouch.

F39   1st Chasseurs d'Afrique, 1841.
      Trooper. Cap: red; black leather peak; tricolour cockade; red pompon. Tunic: light blue; yellow cuffs and collar; white metal buttons and shoulder scales. Red cap lines. Red trousers with black false boots. White belts and gloves.

F

37

38

39

of the soldier had come again in France.

There were other links with the historic past. The great marshals of Napoleon's army had died one by one and for the most part in honour and favour, until only Soult lived on in France. An infantry corporal when the first Revolution occurred, he filled out the last years of the Orleanist monarchy as a Minister of State and President of the Council, and retired to enjoy his peerage and rank of Marshal-General. He died in 1851, aged eighty-two. The last of them, Marmont, died the following year in an exile which had lasted since 1830. Like Napoleon, he had learned his trade in the artillery under the eighteenth-century French masters, and deserted the Emperor only at the end. Having subsequently taken the salt of the restored Bourbons, and been given a major-generalship in the Royal Guard, and high office in the civil state to boot, he found no place in the new order of things when they were deposed.

Meanwhile, the heir to all this made his plans and insisted on discharging his office in military uniform as his four-year term of presidency drew to a close. Before it did so, he had carried out a *coup d'état* with the aid of the obedient troops. Blood was shed, and nine thousand resisters were subsequently deported to Algiers. Deliberately, the day chosen for the long-prepared coup was 2nd December, the anniversary of Austerlitz!

F40 Artillery, 1840.
Gunner, first class. Shako: blue; black peak, lower band, chinstrap; tricolour cockade; red lace top band, chevron, plume, lines; brass badge. Coatee: blue; brass buttons; all distinctives red. Blue trousers with red stripe. White gloves and belts.

F41 Chasseurs d'Orleans, 1845.
Chasseur. Shako: dark blue; yellow lace and piping; dark green pompon or plume; black peak and lower band; tricolour cockade. Tunic: blue, yellow piping; green epaulettes; white metal buttons. Trousers: blue-grey; yellow stripe. Black belt, gaiters, boots.

F42 Infantry, 1849.
Grenadier in campaign dress. Shako: oilcloth cover; double red pompon; black leather peak and strap. Coat: blue-grey; red epaulettes; brass buttons. Red trousers, white gaiters, black boots. Black leather equipment, brass buckles. Hide pack. Tent and pole.

40

41

42

The Second Empire, 1852-70

The Empire was proclaimed on 1st December 1852, and on the following day, an anniversary now of double significance, Napoleon III entered Paris for the first time in that capacity. The symbols of the First Empire were restored to the army, and other and more material favours were bestowed upon it. Nevertheless, it remained the obedient servant and not the master of the state, for this Napoleon was not a genuine man of the tents.

In 1854 the Imperial Guard was re-established. Initially it consisted of two regiments of Grenadiers (F43), two of Voltigeurs (F44), and a battalion of Chasseurs à Pied (F45), together with artillery and cavalry. The latter had two regiments only at first, neither of which was an exact counterpart of any regiment of the original. There had been a corps of elite cavalry for bodyguard duties since 1854, designated Guides. Its instigator and first commander was a Colonel Fleury, who had been one of the most active promoters of the scheme to resurrect the Guard. His regiment was now given Guard status, and wore a hussar uniform. (Cap: black fur; red bag; white-over-black plume. Jacket and pelisse, when worn: green; red collar and cuffs; golden-yellow lace, piping, aiguillettes etc. Red breeches, double yellow stripe. White belts and gloves. Black boots and pouch.) It was partnered by a cuirassier regiment, dressed in the traditional uniform. (Steel helmet without turban; white plume and tuft; black mane. Steel cuirass. Coat: blue; scarlet turned-back tails of the old fashion; scarlet collar; white epaulettes, gauntlets, belts, breeches, aiguillettes. Black jacked boots.)

The Guard was increased in subsequent years. A second regiment of Cuirassiers was formed in 1855 with sky-blue coats,

F43   Guard Grenadiers, 1854.
          Grenadier, full dress. The details for this uniform are as for F1, except for a red collar and red trousers with a blue stripe, light-striped greatcoat roll ornamented on the ends with grenade badges. The front view is as for F44.

F44   Guard Voltigeurs, 1854
          Private, full dress. Shako: blue; black peak and lower band; brass fittings; white cords; yellow lace top band and chevron; tricolour cockade; yellow-over-red plume. Coatee: blue; white lapels; yellow collar and turnbacks; red epaulettes with yellow top rim to fringes; yellow piping; brass buttons. The rear view as for F43, but horn badges instead of grenades on turnbacks and pouch. Remainder of uniform as for F43.

F

43

44

31

and one of Dragoons in the following year which, naturally, assumed the title 'The Empress's'. (Helmet as for Cuirassiers. Coatee: green styled as F35; white lapels, cuffs, turnbacks, epaulettes, aiguillettes, belts; red collar. Red trousers, double green stripe, black false boots.) Lancers and Chasseurs à Cheval also made their appearance, and much later, Carabiniers.

The Guard infantry was augmented by a regiment of Zouaves, formed in the Crimea in 1855. Like most other innovations in the French army in this era, the ancestry of this regiment lay in Algeria, where in Louis Philippe's reign three regiments had been raised of Frenchmen dressed in Arab mode. Two more had been added in 1852, and they and the Chasseurs of the Line supplied picked recruits to the Guard Zouaves (F46).

In short, this was not a slavish imitation of the former Imperial Guard, and the drift away from mere romanticism was marked by the adoption of new tunics by the Foot Guards in 1860 (F48).

The composition of the cavalry remained substantially the same under the Empire as under Louis Philippe, the most notable difference being the disappearance from the line of the two regiments of Carabiniers when the single regiment was included in the Guard in 1865. The Cuirassiers continued to be the epitome of the martial virtues of the earlier Napoleon's army, preserving a continuity of uniform which was not disturbed by the new jacket of 1859 (F50). So for the most part did the Dragoons, who had resumed an approximation of their

F45 Guard Chasseurs à Pied, 1856.
Chasseur in full dress. Shako: blue; black peak, lower band and chinstrap; yellow lace top band and chevron; black plume. Tunic: blue; piped yellow; green epaulettes, brass buttons. Grey-blue trousers, piped yellow. Brown leather leggings with white gaiters. Black belts and boots, grey-blue greatcoat roll, hide pack.

F46 Guard Zouaves, 1856.
Zouave in full dress. Head-dress: red cap; yellow tassel; white turban. Blue jacket and waistcoat; yellow lace and piping; red cuffs. Red trousers, piped yellow. Remainder as F45.

F47 1st Cuirassiers of the Guard, 1859.
Trumpeter in full dress. Helmet: brass; white plume and tuft, red mane. Tunic: blue; white lace, epaulettes, aiguillettes; white metal buttons; red collar, button flap, turnbacks. White belts, gauntlets, breeches. Black jacked boots. Red shabraque with white band. Gold and scarlet trumpet banner.

45

46

47

33

original helmet (see F15) in 1840, but had adopted the red breeches and false boots (see F50) in 1854. The coatee, green with red epaulettes (F35), was subject to regimental distinctions as follows:

Regiment	Lapels	Collar	Cuffs
1st	white	white	green
2nd	white	white	white
3rd	white	green	green
4th	white	green	white
5th	yellow	yellow	green
6th	yellow	yellow	yellow
7th	yellow	green	green
8th	yellow	green	yellow
9th	red	red	green
10th	red	red	red
11th	red	green	green
12th	red	green	red

However, they lost the green jacket which was so much a part of their tradition in 1867, wearing instead a single-breasted plain blue jacket with white collar patches and cuff flaps, and with red epaulettes.

The same pressure to accept standardisation was applied also to the highly individualistic Hussars, who managed to retain their separately coloured jackets until 1869, with a pelisse of the same colour. Shako, cuffs and trousers were red for the 1st, 3rd, 5th and 7th Regiments (except that the 7th had a green shako), and sky-blue for the 2nd, 4th and 8th (but the 2nd had red trousers). Regulations of 1860 replaced the shako by black wool caps, and decreed the wide red breeches for all piped in the jacket colours. The pelisse was abolished in 1862. Finally, a sky-blue tunic with only six rows of braid was ordered as the standard Hussar dress, but this change was overtaken by the war of 1870 before it could be fully implemented.

The infantry suffered some important changes of organisation and of uniform. The Light Infantry regiments were converted to normal infantry in 1854, leaving the Chasseurs à Pied to fill the specialised role of light troops, and the Grenadier and Voltigeur companies of line battalions were abolished in 1868.

These measures necessitated minor modifications of uniform detail, but a fundamental alteration of the infantry uniform took place in 1860 when the style worn by the Chasseurs à Pied of the Guard was decreed for all the line infantry (see F45). There were differences, of course: the shako was all leather, but with the same yellow lace—since yellow was now to be the infantry colour—and an upright, short plume. The line tunic had a yellow collar, and normal infantry had a traditional type of cuff with a yellow button flap. Grenadiers and Voltigeurs wore their respective red and yellow epaulettes, and centre companies green with red piping. Their trousers were red. Chasseurs retained their distinctives (see F41).

Seven years later an equally radical restyling was ordered for the line. Normal infantry received a red felt shako decorated with a blue band and piping (a stiffer version of F53) and tri-colour cockade. When the flank companies disappeared, all wore a double pompon, the upper one being red and the lower one of the battalion colour (1st—dark blue, 2nd—red, 3rd—yellow). The new tunic was as for F51 and F52, dark blue with yellow collar piped dark blue, yellow piping, brass buttons and red epaulettes. The trousers were narrower (F53).

Chasseurs à Pied wore a similar shako of blue, with yellow piping, and green single pompon. The tunic was of the same pattern, with dark blue collar piped yellow, green epaulettes piped yellow and the chevron-style cuff piping (F45). Their trousers were blue-grey with yellow piping down the outside seam. The belt-buckle of the Chasseur equipment was of the open type, not that illustrated in F53, otherwise the equipment was the same.

By this time the number of Zouave line regiments stood at four, and these retained their Arabian fashions unchanged. One might also note the brief existence of a regiment of Swiss, which was raised for service in the Crimea but too late to par-ticipate in the campaign. It was transferred to Africa still in its rifle-green uniforms, to become by a piece of political favouritism the 1st Regiment, Foreign Legion. The unit fought in Algeria and Italy, and was disbanded in 1861.

This, then, was the appearance of the army with which the government of Napoleon III waged whatever battles were con-sidered necessary to achieve the intended aim of making the French presence felt in the diplomacy and economics of Europe and beyond. Although conscription theoretically included all Frenchmen, in practice selection by lottery and exemption by purchase of substitutes excluded most from the seven-year service. The result was a long-service, professional army in-adequately backed by trained manpower reserves, and drawn from the less-favoured sections of society.

Nevertheless, it did what was required of it. It attracted ad-miration in the Crimea, garrisoned Rome, drove the Austrians out of Italy by costly victories at Magenta and Solferino, furthered French interests in Syria and China, pushed the flag onward in Algeria, New Caledonia and Senegal, and opened up a promising new field of colonisation in Indo-China. Only once had it failed to deliver the goods—the attempt to establish a European monarchy in Mexico in 1862-7, where thirty thousand French soldiers campaigned to produce nothing but a sacred relic for the Legion—the wooden hand of Captain Danjou. (He had lost the original at Magenta, and in Mexico commanded a Legion detachment which fought to the last against overwhelming odds at Camerone on 30th April 1863. The last six effectives fixed bayonets when they had fired their last rounds, and charged about 1,700 Mexicans! On the anniversary the Captain's hand is ceremonially paraded, and a description of the battle read to every Legion unit, while the ashes of the Camerone dead are held in honour by each of the Legion chapels in turn.)

It may not have been an army in which the majority of Frenchmen were happy to serve, but they did not repudiate the gifts it brought home. In 1865 Napoleon announced:
'With pride we shall be able to inscribe on a new triumphal arch these words: "To the glory of the French armies for the victories won in Europe, Asia, Africa and America".'
Once again Paris had become the self-appointed capital of Europe.

In 1870 this was challenged from across the Rhine. The appearance of the Prussian army as a factor in the game had caused some reconsideration of its own system by the French government. An attempt was made to create an equivalent of the Prussian reserve of manpower, the Landwehr, by requiring wider conscript service, part of which would be spent in the ultimate pool of trained men, the Garde Mobile. This aroused

F48   Grenadiers of the Guard, 1870.
        Grenadier in field-service dress. Cap: blue; red edge, grenade badge on front, tassel. Tunic: blue; red collar, epaulettes, cuffs, piping; white button flap, lace; brass buttons. Red trousers with wide blue stripe. White gaiters and waistbelt. Remainder of equipment as F53, F54 with black straps as shown.

F49   2nd Hussars, 1870.
        Trooper. Cap: black lambswool; green boss; brass chinscales. Tunic: brown, red collar and cuffs; white lace; white metal buttons. Red breeches with white stripes, black false boots. White belts.

F50   1st Cuirassiers, 1870.
        Trooper. Helmet: steel, brass comb and fittings, red plume and tuft, black mane. Tunic: blue, red collar, turnbacks, piping and cuff button flap; white epaulettes and aiguillettes; white metal buttons. Steel cuirass with brass fittings, black strap. White belts, slings, gloves. Red breeches, blue stripe on outside seams; black false boots.

48

49

50

such opposition among the more vocal sections of French manhood that the Garde Mobile was whittled down to a liability to a brief period of annual training for those who had purchased exemption. On the eve of the Franco-Prussian War, the French war minister boasted that the army was ready 'to the last gaiter-button'. It was not, and the Prussians won.

The Second Republic, 1870-1940

The French government declared war on the Prussians on 15th July. On 2nd August the French army moving forward stormed Saarbrucken. On 4th August the Germans counter-attacked successfully. On 2nd September the Emperor, Marshal MacMahon (a former Legion commander) and their army of 84,000 men became prisoners of war after the disaster of Sedan. On 4th September the Republic was proclaimed. On 1st March 1871 the German army made a triumphant march through Paris.

Defective commanders and inferior artillery had ruined an army of brave soldiers, and the government which had committed the folly of sending it to war vanished overnight.

The Imperial Guard was disbanded within two months of the Emperor's capture, and at this time Lancers also disappeared from the line.

In due course a provisional government emerged to make peace, and one of its first acts was to bring defiant Paris to heel —a task for a French army brought up to strength by the early release of prisoners of war and commanded by Mac-Mahon. It fought its way into the city over the bodies of twenty thousand Parisians, as many as the French dead at Sedan. At this time two young Frenchmen were embarking on their military studies. One, Joseph Joffre, would command the armies of France in 1914. The other, Ferdinand Foch, would command them in 1918. At the latter's request, he was commissioned into the artillery in order to follow the example of his idol, Napoleon I.

F51, F52 The 1867 tunic.
           See text.

F53, F54 Infantryman, 1870.
           Campaign dress. Cap: red top, blue band and piping, black peak, regiment's number in red on band front. Coat: dark blue-grey; brass buttons; red patches on side of collar; red epaulettes. Red trousers, white gaiters. Light blue neck-scarf. Black equipment belts with brass buckles. White haversack; hide pack; khaki bivouac tent strapped to pack.

F

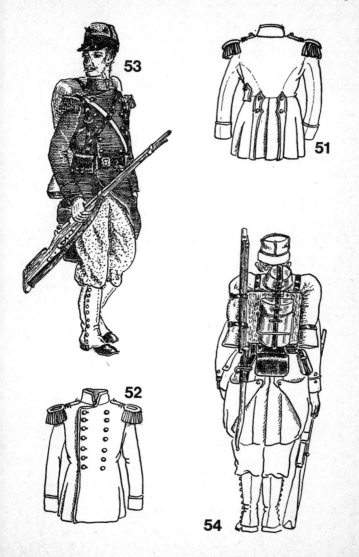

53

51

52

54

The army these men helped to mould in the meanwhile took to heart the challenge to its professionalism posed by the events they witnessed. To avoid a repetition, the defects of 1870 were remedied. The education of commanders was raised to considerable heights. Staff organisation and planning were perfected. Universal conscription ensured adequate manpower reserves and of better calibre. In 1889 the army adopted the Lebel, the first magazine rifle, and in 1897 the 75mm quick-firing field gun which still had no equal in 1914. Above all, it armed itself with what it thought was the essence of the Napoleonic method: attack! Spiced with active service in Africa, Indo-China, and Madagascar, it had recovered its confidence by the century's end, and much of its reputation. Moreover, the assumption of the bully's role by the German government put the French army on the side of the angels at last.

All this was reflected in the continuing trend towards utility of the uniforms, the principal forms of which are illustrated. Dragoons wore a plain blue tunic with white collar and button flaps, red collar numerals, and white metal buttons, together with a blue neck-scarf, red breeches with a blue stripe, and their traditional helmet which was covered in the field. Chasseurs à Cheval wore a sky-blue tunic and low shako, white metal buttons, red collar and button flap, and a double sky-blue stripe on their red breeches. Hussars wore a braided sky-

F55, F56   1899 infantry tunic.
Blue; blue collar patches; red collar, epaulettes, button flaps, collar numerals, skirt piping; brass buttons. (Worn with 1886 kepi, like F53 but with cockade, badge and battalion pompon, red trousers, white gaiters.)

F57   Chasseurs à Pied, 1910.
Chasseur in Guard Order. Cap: blue; yellow piping; green pompon; tricolour cockade; brass horn badge; black peak, chinstrap. Tunic: blue; white metal buttons; yellow numerals on collar; green epaulettes piped yellow; light blue neck-scarf. Black equipment; brass belt plate. Blue trousers. White gaiters.

F58   12th Cuirassiers, 1914.
Lieutenant in campaign dress. Helmet: covered with khaki cloth. Tunic: blue; collar piped red; red button flap; silver epaulettes, buttons, collar numerals, double rank bands on cuffs. Steel cuirass, brass fittings, black strap, red lining. Red breeches, blue stripe. Black boots, glasses and map cases. Tan gloves.

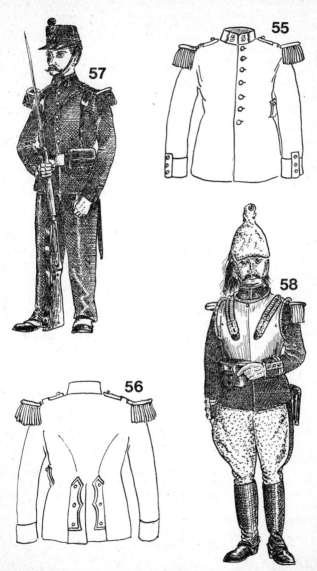

F

55

57

56

58

blue tunic. Even so, the French still lagged behind the Germans in this respect, and not only behind such a professionally worthy opponent, but also the amateurish and despised (by both Germans and French) British army.

When the war came, however, the disasters of Sedan and Metz were not repeated. It was the German government which declared war in 1914, and the German army which attacked on a strictly ordered timetable plan which had lain ready for the event since 1905—the Schlieffen Plan. Although the French Plan XVII, based upon the doctrine of attack, disintegrated at the moment of execution, Joffre kept his head and his soldiers their courage. In the retreat from the frontier, they outmanoeuvred and eventually outfought their enemy, and turning at bay along the river Marne barely a month after the opening shots were exchanged, inflicted upon the Germans what was in retrospect seen to be the decisive defeat of the war.

The German acknowledgement of that defeat was still four years and several million dead away, 1,500,000 of them French. The lines of trenches which produced the deadlock were dug in French soil for the most part, and it was chiefly French villages and towns which were devastated by the conflict. Along this line, in the spring of 1915, the dark blue and red of the French army was replaced by 'horizon blue', and later that year the kepi by the steel helmet (see F61). Chasseurs continued to wear blue with blackened helmets to the war's end.

The efforts to expel the invader imposed unprecedented hardships upon the line soldiers, but it was not this which almost broke the French army in 1917 and drove it to open mutiny. After all, the soldiers of each of the armies involved suffered

F59 Infantryman, 1914.
Campaign dress. As for F53 and F54, except that kepi covered with blue-grey, no epaulettes, and black leather gaiters. Pack covered with grey or unbleached cloth. (Chasseurs à Pied wore blue kepi, piped yellow, and blue-grey trousers.)

F60 Artillery, 1914.
Brigadier (NCO) in campaign dress. Blue throughout, with red kepi-piping, cuff rank-braid, breeches' stripes. Light blue neck-scarf. Natural leather belts. Black boots and kepi peak.

F61 Infantryman, 1917.
Horizon-blue throughout, including the buttons, but helmet slightly darker. Equipment as for F59, but in natural leather.

F

59

60

61

as much. But French soldiers had to endure neglect of simple needs, indifference to their fate or the fate of their families, contempt from politicians and intellectuals, inflammatory propaganda from demagogues on the make—the legacy of one hundred years of French politics. Little wonder that they doubted the value of their sacrifices, even if many of these things were mended in time.

Strong allies were at hand to take on the burden of harassing the enemy, the final advance to victory being co-ordinated under the hand of a Frenchman, the newly created Marshal of France, Ferdinand Foch. The peace conference met in Paris, and the treaty was signed in the very Hall of Mirrors at Versailles where the vainglorious German Empire had been proclaimed in 1871. It was a symbolic moment of triumph, but it was dearly bought, and it was not the last word.

Between the wars, the moral rot of French politics deepened, and defeatism in the army became even more pronounced. Outwardly it was once again the arbiter of Europe's destiny, behind which frightened British politicians, among others, were glad to shelter their electors to whom they could not or would not tell the truth. Inwardly, however, the French army was, and knew itself to be, the army of 1917. Khaki replaced horizon blue in 1935, but the basic uniform was the same. The concrete and steel of the Maginot Line replaced the trenches in the earth, but the basic lack of will remained unchanged.

Consequently, when the next war against Germany began in 1939, an army of sixty-three divisions (with five British) stood by while the Germans imposed their will on Eastern Europe.

F62 General Officer, 1917.
Kepi: red top, blue band, gold lace and piping, black peak. Horizon-blue uniform, including buttons. Double dark-blue breeches' stripes. Black boots and belts.

F63 Foreign Legion, 1939.
Legionnaire, first class. Kepi: white cover, black peak. Coat: khaki, brass buttons, green rank-chevrons on sleeves and lapels, green grenade badge on lapels. White scarf. Brown leather equipment. Khaki drill trousers, unbleached puttees, black boots.

F64 The grenade badge of the Legion.

F65 The 1939 kepi.
Dark blue, madder-red top, black peak, gold badge and false strap (always worn with the white cover, until the rank of caporal-chef is reached, when the cover is discarded).

F

62

63

64

65

When the Germans eventually attacked in the West eight months later, the French army crumbled before them even more swiftly than in 1870, and France became an economic province in the German New Order.

A year later, June 1942, Frenchmen met Germans again in battle. The place was Bir Hacheim, a defended 'box' on the left flank of the British line opposing Rommel in the Libyan desert. The defenders were the 1st Free French Brigade, a mixture of units formed in one or two colonies, troops who escaped from France via Dunkirk, and a vital core of two understrength Legion battalions. General Koenig's defence of the 'box' is a military epic in its own right. First against Italian armour, and then against the Afrika Korps with full air support, he held Bir Hacheim for fifteen days' continuous assault, and having carried out the task assigned to him by the British, withdrew in his own time. It was a step on the way back to military respectability.

THE GERMAN ARMY

Strictly speaking, it is not possible to consider the existence of a completely unified German army until 1919. Until then there were the troops of the several states which made up the largely geographical expression 'Germany'. One of these states was the Kingdom of Prussia, and the Prussian army was the instrument by which united Germany was made a fact, with fateful results for France, Europe and the world.

Prussia was a state without natural frontiers, created out of the original family estates of the Hohenzollerns. Survival depended upon a strong army, and the foundations of this were laid by King Frederick William I (1688-1740). Compulsory military service was introduced for all but those in occupations which might be considered essential for war-waging, such as industrial craftsmen. Such service was for life, since trained men returned to their civilian jobs but were regarded as a reserve liable to recall. The Officer Corps was drawn from the landowners (Junkers) who served as a social duty, but equal attention was lavished upon the military education of high-quality rankers who formed the body of NCOs. As the guarantor of the state's existence, the army was given a privileged position in the state and closely identified with the person of the monarch. As Prussia was a poor state in economic terms, all ranks knew how to cultivate Spartan virtues and were therefore ideal material for soldiering.

This army was used to good effect by his son, Frederick 'the Great' (1712-86), who is ranked among the world's great cap-

46

tains. A good theoretician and field commander, he had a preference for short, decisive wars: they were less costly to a poor country. Hence, he chose the offensive, attempted to keep the initiative, and regarded the enemy's army as the prime target, not the mere occupation of territory.

This was the Prussian system, and the reader will see its influence in the following pages, right up to 1940. The French received their first check from it in Frederick the Great's own day, and it had been invoked only half-heartedly against the Revoultion in its early stages. In October 1806 it faced the armies of Napoleon at Jena and Auerstadt and was completely overwhelmed! By the subsequent Treaty of Paris (1808), the Prussian army was reduced to 42,000 at the dictation of the victorious French, as previously, by the Treaty of Tilsit, Prussian territory had been reduced by half. The consequences of this brutality were to rebound upon French heads for the next century and a half.

The recovery of Prussia, 1807-15

The Prussian government wasted no time, but set up a board of inquiry to recommend reforms, on which board appeared such names as Scharnhorst, Gneisenau, and Clausewitz. Among other measures, the fierce discipline of the old army was replaced by the deliberate cultivation of a sense of duty and patriotism in the ranks, and attention paid to devices for expanding the small army in wartime by passing trained men more quickly into reserve categories. The work was not interrupted by the obligation to supply Prussian troops to Napoleon's Moscow campaign.

The cavalry of the new army consisted of nineteen regiments, which contained some designated Guard units. The cuirassier regiments wore the uniform G5, with differenced colour piping, collar, cuffs and tail trimming.

Regiment	Facings	Buttons
No. 1, Silesian Cuirassiers	Black	yellow metal
No. 2, East Prussian Cuirassiers	Light blue	white metal
No. 3, Garde du Corps (Bodyguard)	Red	white metal
No. 4, Brandenburg Cuirassiers	Blue (dark until 1813, then corn-flower).	yellow metal

The 3rd Regiment wore the Guard Star (G4) on their helmets instead of the Prussian eagle and Guard cuff and collar lace (see G1, G2, G9), and on campaign the Cuirassiers wore the tunic shown in G12. This had white shoulder-straps in each case, but collar and piping on the top edge of the cuff were in the correct facing colour (but red for 4th).

The Dragoons wore the uniform G7, except the Normal Dragoon Squadron, which was a picked Guard unit and wore the Guard Star and shako (G7) and Guard lace. Dragoons also wore the campaign tunic G12, with collar and shoulder straps of the facing colour.

Regiment	Facings	Buttons and shako badge
No. 1 Queen's Dragoons	crimson	white metal
No. 2 1st West Prussian Dragoons	white	white metal
No. 3 Lithuanian Dragoons	scarlet	yellow metal
No. 4 2nd West Prussian Dragoons	scarlet	white metal
No. 5 Brandenburg Dragoons	black	yellow metal
No. 6 Neumark Dragoons	rose	white metal
Normal Dragoon Squadron	red	yellow metal
Two more regiments were added in 1815:		
No. 7 Rhine Dragoons	white	yellow metal
No. 8 Magdeburg Dragoons	yellow	white metal

The Normal Dragoon Squadron was formed in 1811, drawing on the heavy cavalry regiments, and the same time a Normal Hussar Squadron was brought into being. Hussars wore the uniform G6, troopers having white fur on the pelisse, NCOs black, and officers grey (but all ranks of the Normal Squadron had black). Girdles were parti-coloured in the colours of the facings and the buttons. The Life Hussars had the death's head badge on their shakos instead of the large national cockade, and the Normal Squadron had the Guard star.

Regiment	Jacket and pelisse	Cuffs and collars	Buttons and lace
No. 1 1st Life Hussars	black	scarlet (white shoulder straps)	white

G1 The Guard Lancer Squadron, 1813.
Lancer in parade dress. Lance cap: leather; dark blue cloth top piped with yellow cord; yellow cap lines; black and white pompon; black feather plume. Jacket: dark blue; scarlet collar, cuffs, piping and tail trim; yellow lace on collar and cuffs; yellow metal buttons and shoulder-scales; white epaulettes. Blue and red girdle. Black leather shoulder-belt. Overalls: dark grey, reinforced with leather.

G2 The Guard Cossack Squadron, 1813.
Trooper in parade dress. Cap: black bearskin; white plume and hangings; red bag. Jacket: dark blue; collar and cuffs piped red, with white lace. Overalls: dark blue, with double red stripe on outside seams. White girdle, covering black sword-belt with slings. Black leather sword-knot.

G3 Shako of the Normal Dragoon Squadron.
Black leather, yellow metal fittings, white plume.

G4 The Guard Star.

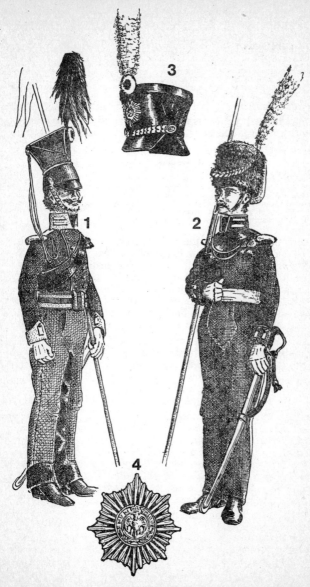

Regiment	Jacket and pelisse	Cuffs and collars	Buttons and lace
No. 2 2nd Life Hussars	black	scarlet (scarlet shoulder straps)	white
No. 3 Brandenburg Hussars	dark blue	scarlet	white
No. 4 1st Silesian Hussars	brown	scarlet	white
No. 5 Pomeranian Hussars	dark blue	dark blue	yellow
No. 6 2nd Silesian Hussars	green	scarlet	yellow
Normal Hussar Squadron	dark blue	scarlet	yellow

In 1815 additional regiments were added, based upon volunteer units which were raised after 1813, when Prussia joined in the war against Napoleon:

Regiment	Jacket and pelisse	Cuffs and collars	Buttons and lace
No. 7 West Prussian Hussars	black	red	yellow
No. 8 1st Westphalian Hussars	dark blue	light blue	white
No. 9 Rhine Hussars	light blue	light blue	yellow
No. 10 1st Magdeburg Hussars	green	light blue	yellow
No. 11 2nd Westphalian Hussars	green	red	white
No. 12 2nd Magdeburg Hussars	light blue	light blue	white

Lancers (Uhlans) wore the uniform G11, together with a shako as for G6 with yellow hangings. At this stage the only unique features of Lancer dress were the girdle and 'Polish' cuff, but the Life Lancer Squadron formed in 1808 adopted an Austrian style of uniform which included the lance cap. Two years later, they were redesignated the Guard Lancer Squadron, changing to the dress of the line with the lance cap as before (G1), and they alone carried on their lances pennons in the

G5   The Brandenburg Cuirassier Regiment, 1813.
     Trooper in parade dress. Helmet: black leather; brass fittings; black hair crest. Coat: white; blue collar, cuffs, shoulder-strap piping and tail trim. (For rear, see G13.) White sword and shoulder belts, gloves. Grey overalls.

G6   The Brandenburg Hussar Regiment, 1812.
     Hussar. Shako: black leather; white hangings; pompon as G1, Prussian national cockade of black and white. Jacket: dark blue; scarlet collar and cuffs; braiding and piping, white (for rear, see G14, right). Pelisse: the same, white fur (for rear, G14, left). Girdle: white and scarlet. Shoulder and sword belts, black. Sabretache, red with white edges. White gloves. Grey overalls.

G7   The Neumark Dragoon Regiment, 1813.
     Dragoon in parade dress. Shako: black leather; white metal fittings and eagle; white hangings; Prussian pompon; white 'busch'. Coat: light blue; rose collar; cuffs; shoulder straps; tail trim (G13); white metal buttons. White gloves, belts. Grey overalls.

5

6

7

G

Polish national colours (white over red) which were the later hallmark of lancers in other armies. Those of the line regiments were the colours of their respective provinces.

Regiment	Shoulder-straps	Pennons
No. 1 West Prussian Lancers	white	white over blue
No. 2 Silesian Lancers	scarlet	red over blue
No. 3 Brandenburg Lancers	yellow	yellow over blue

In 1815, the pennon colours were changed to the Prussian national colours—white over black.

The Guard Cossack Squadron (G2) was raised in 1813, and together with the other Guard squadrons constituted the Guard Light Cavalry Regiment. In 1815 the squadrons were expanded to create Guard Dragoon, Guard Hussar, and Guard Lancer regiments, the Cossacks being attached to the Lancers.

The status and distinction of the infantry regiments are less easy to tabulate, because as well as having a seniority in the line the regiments were also grouped in provincial brigades, and had a seniority within the brigade. There was a further complication: the initial establishment of a regiment in 1808 was two musketeer battalions, one fusilier (light infantry) battalion, and two grenadier companies which were detached and grouped into grenadier battalions at the disposal of the brigade. There were also Foot Guards, an elite ('Normal') battalion,

G8   Musketeer, Line Infantry, parade dress, 1815.
   Shako: black leather; white band; Prussian pompon; royal cypher FWR in brass. Coat: dark blue; collar and cuffs (provincial colour, see text); shoulder-straps (seniority colour, see text); red turnbacks on coat tails; blue flap on cuff (the 'Brandenburg cuff'); yellow metal buttons. Equipment: white belts, hide pack, black leather cartridge-box, grey greatcoat, short sabre on left. Trousers: white in summer, grey in winter. Black gaiters.

G9   1st Foot Guards, officer, parade dress, 1812.
   Shako: gold lace band, gilt fittings, black cock's feather plume, Guard Star and Prussian pompon. Coat: dark blue, scarlet shoulder-straps edged with silver lace; scarlet collar and cuffs (the 'Swedish cuff') with silver lace; scarlet turnbacks to tails; silver buttons. Silver sash, with two black stripes. White gloves. Grey overalls, red stripe with yellow metal buttons down seam.

G10   Drummer, Line Infantry, campaign dress, 1815.
   As G8. Shako covered with black oil cloth cover. Drummer's 'swallow's nests' in provincial colour edged with white lace. Brass drum, white cords, white- and red-patterned bands.

8

9

10

and riflemen (Jäger and Schützen). It must be remembered that the infantry structure was merely to provide a framework within the political limitations of the enforced peace upon which a much larger wartime army might be built. Nevertheless, dress distinctions existed for all these categories.

The basic uniform was that of the musketeer (G8). Fusiliers wore the same uniform, but different shako decorations (see G16: the fusilier busch was black, and NCOs had the bottom quarter coloured white), the busch being replaced by a plume (G22) in 1813. Grenadiers wore the G8 uniform, with the black busch or later plume but the Prussian heraldic eagle as a shako badge (see G7). Musicians wore 'swallow's nests' shoulder distinctives (G10); these were in the provincial colour, and if entitled to wear a busch, it was red. NCOs wore lace on the collar and cuffs (e.g. G11).

The collar and cuffs of line regiments were in the provincial colour: East Prussia—brick-red, Brandenburg—scarlet, West Prussia—crimson, Silesia—lemon-yellow, Pomerania—white, Magdeburg—light blue. (Westphalia—rose, and Rhine—crab red were added in 1814 to the original six provincial brigades.)

The shoulder-strap colour indicated the seniority within the brigade: 1st Regiment—white, 2nd—scarlet, 3rd—yellow, 4th—light blue. The G8 cuff was known as the 'Brandenburg' cuff, and it was customary to leave the bottom button of the flap undone.

As opportunity permitted, the Guard was increased. There was one regiment in 1808, which wore a white busch (G17) and shoulder-strap, and red collar and 'Swedish' cuffs (G9) with Guard lace. A second regiment of Foot Guards was formed in 1813, based upon the 'Normal' battalion, and was distinguished by a 'Brandenburg' cuff (G8). The following year, the grenadier battalions of the brigades were transformed into two Guard Grenadier Regiments: No. 1 'Czar Alexander' and No. 2 'Kaiser Franz', in honour of the Russian and Austrian allies

G11 The West Prussian Lancer Regiment, 1813.
   NCO in campaign dress. Shako: black cover, beneath as for G6 with yellow hangings. Jacket: dark blue; scarlet collar, cuffs (the 'Polish cuff') and tail trim; NCO's lace on collar and cuffs; yellow metal buttons; white shoulder-straps. Blue and red girdle. Grey overalls. Black leather belts.

G12 Landwehr (i.e. provincial militia) cavalryman, 1815.
   Shako: black leather; pompon and white Landwehr cross. Tunic: dark blue; collar and shoulder-straps of provincial colour. Black belts. Grey overalls.

G13 Rear view of heavy cavalry coat.

G14 Rear view of Hussar pelisse and dolman.

in the war against Napoleon. These regiments wore a Prussian flying eagle on their shakos instead of the Guard Star, otherwise the only difference was in the shoulder-strap—white with the Czar's cypher in red, and red with the Austrian Emperor's cypher in yellow respectively. They wore the 'Brandenburg' cuff.

At the same time, a Guard Rifle (Schützen) Battalion was formed, to pair the existing Guard Jäger Battalion. Rifle units wore a dark green coatee, with scarlet collar, shoulder-straps and 'Swedish' cuffs, and yellow metal buttons. They wore a shako with a national cockade (as in G16) with green cords and black busch. They wore black belt equipment (as did all Fusilier battalions) and black leather knee-boots. The two Guard Battalions wore the Guard Star on their shakos, and yellow Guard Lace on their collars and cuffs.

The Foot Artillery wore an infantry-type uniform (G8), with scarlet turnbacks, black collars and cuffs piped scarlet, and dark blue button flap. Horse Artillery wore a cavalry coat (G5), with the same colours for collar and cuffs, but dark blue turnbacks, trimmed with black braid. Until 1814 shoulder-straps were white for the Prussian brigade, scarlet for the Brandenburg, and yellow for the Silesian, but thereafter scarlet for all. The shako bore a brass grenade badge (or Guard Star where appropriate), with an upper band which was white for Foot gunners, and yellow for the Horse, which also had yellow cords and cap lines and a white plume in parade order.

In 1812 this nuclear army numbered some 66,000 men, of whom 20,000 were marched off to Russia by Napoleon. Ironically, the expansion of the Prussian army which began at the beginning of 1813 was undertaken at a French 'request', and was accomplished by calling up reserves, organising volunteer units, and finally by calling out all fit men between the ages of seventeen and seventy-four into a militia force, or Landwehr, officered by 'dug-outs' and novices. By these expedients, the strength of the army stood at 271,000 by the summer! It was then, however, fighting against the French. Partially run down after Napoleon's abdication, the Prussian army contributed 117,000 men under Blucher to the final Waterloo campaign.

To equip such a force in the time was, of course, beyond the capability of Prussian industry. Had it been conducted under French control, as the French had intended, the process would have benefited French industry (which in fact was one of the chief purposes of the French army and its conquests, a matter usually overlooked by students of the period). Thus, the Prussians appeared in a variety of uniforms and equipment hastily

THE RECOVERY OF PRUSSIA

supplied by the Austrians and British, or, in the case of the Landwehr, cheap expedients and half-dress. The Silesian Landwehr received 20,000 Austrian muskets which, on inspection, were found to have no touch-holes bored in them!

The two illustrations G12 and G17 are therefore 'according to the regulations', but it should not be assumed that all units were so garbed. The provincial colours for the Landwehr were: East Prussia—orange red, Pomerania—brick red, West Prussia—black, Silesia—yellow, Brandenburg—brick red. (The following were added in 1814: Elbe—light blue, Westphalia—green, Rhine—crab red.)

Other German states, 1807-15

Austria apart, other German states had their individual armies, which yielded contingents to the army of the 'Confederation of the Rhine', the French-dominated organisation which was the Napoleonic solution to the problem of German unity. Bavaria, for example, contributed thirty thousand men. The crested helmet and light blue coatee colour were the distinctive features of their uniforms (see G19 and also G33), although the six Light Infantry battalions wore green coatees and the artillery dark blue. As for the Bavarian cavalry, the two Dragoon regiments wore white coatees with red facings and the four Light Horse regiments green coatees. These were in the style of F19, and were worn with the crested helmet until the cavalry was reorganised in 1811 into six Light Horse regiments. These wore plain green coatees and breeches with either black or poppy-coloured collars, cuffs and turnbacks and shakos. Shortly afterwards, a green-uniformed Lancer regiment with poppy lapels and other facings made its appearance, and a Hussar regiment dressed in light blue with white braiding and other lace, white pelisse, and a white-over-blue plume on the shako. (White and light blue were the state colours, and were also worn on the Lancers' pennons.)

The King of Saxony was another leading German adherent of Napoleon, to whom he owed his title. The Saxon army, apart from a Guard, consisted of eight white-uniformed infantry regiments (G21), and three with green coatees and grey breeches in the Jäger rôle. There were two regiments of Cuirassiers, wearing pale yellow coats until 1810, then white, with a cuirass black-crested brass helmet, together with four Dragoon regiments (shakos, red coatees, white plumes and cap lines, regimental facings) and a Light Dragoon regiment. In addition, there was a single Hussar regiment dressed in a mid-blue Hussar uniform with black collar and cuffs, and white plumes, shako-hangings, and braiding. One of the Dragoon regiments was converted to Lancers in 1811, and wore a blue lance cap.

The Bavarians changed sides well before the Battle of Leipzig (October 1813) and so were numbered among the Allies, but the Saxons left it somewhat late. The battle was at its height when they crossed over and turned their guns on their former comrades.

Some Germans had the merit of having committed themselves against Napoleon from the beginning. The army of Hanover had been disbanded on French orders in 1803, but that state enjoyed unique links with Great Britain through a common ruler, so that many of its members enlisted in the King's German Legion which campaigned in the Peninsula and at Waterloo with the British army. They wore British uniforms and were organised in the British manner. Duke Frederick William of Brunswick-Oels also recruited a corps for the British service, the distinguishing features of which were its all-black uniforms and death's head badges (see G62). The Brunswick riflemen wore a grey uniform, in imitation of Austrian Jäger, and at Waterloo the Corps also possessed Lancers uniformed in the Austrian style with black uniforms and blue distinctives.

These few examples must suffice to illustrate the degree to which French domination of Germany was taken by Napoleon, and the varied resistance individual states were able to offer. The Battle of Leipzig was the culmination of gathering confidence among the states of central and eastern Europe in their ability to throw out the French by united action, the majority of the fighting men being supplied by the Russian, Prussian and Austrian armies. The Peninsular Campaign, Waterloo and the whole of the naval war are not really significant in continental eyes.

G15 General Officer, field service dress, 1815.
     Cap: grey, piped scarlet, black peak. Coat: grey (infantry; artillery and cavalry generals—dark blue) lined and piped scarlet. Sash and overalls as G9. (N.B. from 1815 generals wore a double red stripe on overalls.)
G16 Shako, NCO of line Fusiliers.
     As for G8, but with cockade as G6 and black-over-white busch.
G17 Shako, NCO of 1st Foot Guards.
     As for G16, but with the Guard Star.
G18 Landwehr Infantry, 1813.
     Cap: dark blue; band and piping of provincial colour; white Landwehr cross; Prussian cockade; black peak. Tunic: dark blue; collar, cuffs and usually shoulder-straps of provincial colour. White belts, cloth haversack, trousers. Footwear, various.

15

16

17

18

The rise of the Prussian Empire, 1815-71

The victorious Allies who framed the peace treaty of 1815 were guided more by the need to seal off the French military potential from Central Europe than by any fears that, by strengthening the Prussian state to form an anti-French bastion, they might be creating another military giant to trouble the future. However, this proved in time to be the result of their work.

The rulers of Saxony were 'punished' for their failure to transfer their loyalties earlier by the loss of about half of their territory, which passed to Prussia. At the same time, the Prussian government received the Rhineland and Westphalia as compensation for yielding up two-thirds of its Polish territory to reward the Russians for their efforts. No one foresaw the economic importance of the exchange, for Germany was still chiefly an agricultural country, and the modern industrial complex of the Ruhr was not then in anyone's prospect.

In fact, economics and not war-making served the purpose of Prussian expansion at this time: this book is not the place to discuss the point at length, but the reader should note, if he wishes to appreciate the circumstances of his own times, that there are other ways of pursuing conquest than sending forth

G19 Bavarian Infantryman, 1810.
Helmet: black leather; black fur crest, brass fittings; white-blue-white roundel as the Bavarian state cockade on the left side. Coatee: light blue with red turnbacks on the tails, and piping on the shoulder-straps, cuffs and cuff flaps; cuffs, collar and lapels in regimental colours (e.g. 1st Regiment—red, 8th Regiment—yellow etc.); collar piped white; buttons and lace white or yellow. White waistcoat, breeches, belts and straps. Black gaiters and cartridge pouch on right. Hide pack. Grey overcoat.

G20 The Grand Duchy of Baden, Grenadier of the Guard, 1806.
Bearskin: black; white metal plate; white hangings; white-over-red plume. Coat: blue; red turnbacks, collar and cuffs; white lace and white metal buttons. White belts and breeches. Black gaiters.

G21 Saxon infantry officer, 1810.
Shako: black; gilt fittings; silver hangings; white cockade at base of plume; scarlet plume. Coatee: white, with all facings and tail piping in regimental colours (e.g. 1st— scarlet, 4th blue etc.); gilt buttons and epaulettes; silver gorget. White waistcoat and breeches. Black boots.

19

20

21

the soldiers. He should note, especially, the history of the rise of modern Germany.

Briefly, then, the industrialisation of Germany got under way during this period, and was accompanied by the creation of a Prussian customs union (Zollverein) which had the practical effect of making the Prussian capital, Berlin, the economic capital of the German states which felt obliged to enter the union. Once they accepted economic leadership from Berlin, political leadership inevitably followed, struggle against it though they did. Established in 1834, by 1866 all but a small handful of minor German states had been forced into it.

Little enough was seen of the Prussian army amid these events, or, indeed, those of the other states. In uniform fashions, it was Russia which established the mode (G22) until the 1840s. In 1842 the Prussian army was provided with a more practical uniform, the main features of which were to persist until the middle of the First World War. Despite an undeserved reputation for rigidity and pomp, the Prussian approach to military clothing was much more enlightened than that of other armies in Europe, combining comfort and serviceability with the moral-supporting traditional embellishments in an easy balance. The basis of the change was the adoption of the tunic and the spiked helmet, to be worn by the entire army but for the Hussars (G32) and Lancers (G27).

In the infantry grey trousers with a red stripe down the outside seams were worn in winter dress, and from 1843 a horsehair plume was worn falling from the spike in certain regiments. This was white for Guards, black for Grenadiers and rifle regiments. Rifle regiments also wore a green tunic with

G22 Guard Grenadier Regiment No. 1, Kaiser Alexander.
Private 1828. Shako: black; brass fittings, white hangings; black plume; Prussian cockade. Coatee: dark blue; scarlet collar, cuffs, turnbacks; white shoulder-straps; brass buttons. White straps, trousers. Equipment as G26.

G23 'Swedish' cuff.

G24 Skirts of tunic.

G25 11th Infantry Regiment, senior NCO, 1843.

G26 Private.
Helmet: black; brass fittings; Prussian cockade behind right chinscale boss. Tunic: dark blue; scarlet cuffs, button flaps, collar patches, piping on skirts (G24) and front tunic edge; yellow shoulder-straps; (NCO has rank gold lace on collar and cuffs); brass buttons. White trousers, straps. Brown leather pack, black leather cartridge-pouch, grey greatcoat, metal mess-tin.

G

22

23

24

25

26

black leather belts. The facings were red for Jäger and black for Schützen, with red piping in both cases. The cross-belt equipment was replaced in 1847 by the shoulder-braces, still with the pouch worn in the centre of the back, but in 1850 two pouches worn on the front of the belt were introduced.

In the cavalry Dragoons wore a mid-blue tunic, black leather helmet and a black horsehair plume on parade. The tunic cuffs were of the 'Swedish' type, and facings and pipings were of regimental colours (e.g. crimson facings and white piping for the 3rd Dragoons). Cuirassiers wore white tunics with regimental facings and piping. The artillery wore black leather helmets, with a plume on occasions (although later the spike on the helmet was replaced by a ball), and a dark blue tunic with black facings and a 'Swedish' cuff.

During the wave of revolutions in 1848 various state armies were used against their own people to restore order, in Berlin especially. There was even a little war for the Prussian army against a foreign foe, the enemy being Denmark, and the cause a 'German' one—the declared intent of the Danes to incorporate the duchy of Schleswig in Denmark. It was a half-hearted affair, successful from the purely military point of view,

G27 3rd Lancer Regiment.
    Lancer, 1843. Lance cap: black leather; yellow top piped white, brass eagle and chinscales; white cap lines; Prussian cockade; white plume. Coatee: dark blue; scarlet collar, cuffs, lapels; yellow shoulder-straps with brass crescents; brass buttons. Scarlet and blue girdle. White shoulder-belt, black pouch. White sword slings, gloves. Grey overalls, scarlet stripe on outside seams. Black boots.

G28 2nd Cuirassier Regiment.
    Trooper, 1843. Helmet: white metal; brass edges, eagle, fittings; Prussian cockade behind right chinscale boss. Tunic: white; crimson collar piped white; crimson piping on shoulder straps, seams, skirts (G30), doubled on either side of tunic front. White metal breastplate and back; brass scales; black waistbelt; crimson lining piped white. White shoulder-belt, black pouch. White sword slings, gauntlets. Grey overalls, scarlet stripe on outside seams. Black boots.

G29 General, 1843.
    Hat: black, gold lace, black and white feather plume. Coat: dark blue; scarlet collar, cuffs, turnbacks; gold lace, aiglet, gilt buttons. Silver waist sash. White gloves. Grey overalls, double scarlet stripes. Black boots.

27

29

28

but the Prussian government withdrew from the field under Russian pressure. Continued civil and political turmoil in Germany shortly afterwards brought about a confrontation between the Prussian army and one from Austria, supported by contingents from Bavaria and Württemberg. Some shots were fired, but again the Prussian government retreated from its position. It was still possible for other European governments to subdue any Prussian bid for power in Central Europe.

This situation was altered after 1862, when Bismarck became the Minister-President of Prussia as the result of a political crisis over Roon's proposals for army reform. Roon was the war minister from 1859 to 1871, and his aim was to increase the size of the field army, almost doubling its strength with thirty-nine new infantry regiments and ten of cavalry, by increasing the period and scope of conscription. The size of the Landwehr would be reduced, and it would no longer be regarded as a front-line formation. Most Prussian politicians had no objection to the increase in the field army, but were inclined to wax sentimental over the Landwehr—the 'citizen-army' of Liberal mythology. In the event, with Bismarck manipulating

G30 Garde du Corps.
Gala uniform, 1843. Helmet: brass; white metal star, eagle, edgings; Prussian cockade behind right chinscale boss. Tunic: white, piped scarlet (front as G28). Scarlet breast and back covers, edged white, with white Guard Star on both. White gauntlets, breeches, belts, slings, black pouch, white metal star. Black jacked boots.

G31 1st Foot Guards.
Officer 1843. Cap: gilt front; silver star; white band edged with silver; scarlet crown lined white; silver and black rose; gilt chinscales with eagles behind bosses. Tunic: dark blue; scarlet cuffs, collar patches, piping on skirts (G24) and front edge; silver Guard lace on cuffs and collar; silver buttons; silver shoulder-scales. Silver sash. White gloves, trousers.

G32 The Guard Hussar Regiment.
Officer, 1845. Cap: brown sealskin; scarlet bag, gilt chinscales; silver Guard Star; silver and black national cockade; white plume with black base; silver and black lines. Dolman: all scarlet; gold lace, buttons. Pelisse: dark blue; gold lace, buttons; grey fur. Silver sash, sword knot. White shoulder-belt, black pouch with silver star. White slings, gloves. Sabretache: black, red cover, edged gold with FWR cypher. Grey overalls, scarlet stripe on outside seams. Black boots.

30

31

32

the politics, Roon got his way, which included an increased budget to re-equip the army with the latest weapons.

Behind him was the Chief of the General Staff, Moltke, who hailed from Mecklenburg and had followed his father into the Danish army. Entering Prussian service in 1822, he had worked his way to the top without having any campaign experience. Nevertheless, he was a highly successful head of the organisation which was to be the biggest single factor in the future success of the army. The General Staff planned and trained in peacetime for possible wars, studied options through wargames and manoeuvres, and positioned its members throughout the entire army structure, so that the army moved as one. Yet under Moltke, who did not believe in blind obedience to preconceived orders, it did not discourage initiative in the field.

There followed a series of wars, in which the army answered instantly to the demands made upon it by the not altogether well-directed diplomacy of Bismarck, ensuring the reputations of them both and Prussian ascendency in Europe.

The Danes succeeded in producing uproar in Germany over Schleswig-Holstein again in 1863, and it was Hanoverian and Saxon troops who were first across the frontier at Christmas to save the duchies 'for Germany'. Prussian troops followed later, less altruistically, with the Austrians in tow to give a

G33 Bavarian infantryman, 1870.
Helmet: black; black fur crest; black chinstrap; brass fittings. Tunic: light blue; red piping and shoulder 'wings'; collar and cuffs of regimental colour (e.g. 5th Regiment— rose); white metal buttons. Trousers: pale blue with red stripe on outside seams. Black leather equipment and boots, brass buckles. Dark grey greatcoat roll.

G34 Saxon infantryman, 1866.
Cap: pale blue; piped red; black leather peak and strap, band of brigade colour (e.g. 4th Infantry Brigade—white). Tunic: pale blue, piped red; collar and cuffs of brigade colour; brass buttons. Trousers: pale blue with red stripe on outside seams. Black leather equipment and boots.

G35 Wurttemberger infantryman, 1870.
Cap: blue; red piping around top; red lace below state cockade held with white metal button; black leather peak and strap. Tunic: blue; red piping, collar, shoulder straps and 'wings'; collar patches of regimental colour (e.g. 4th Regiment—green); white metal buttons. Trousers: dark grey with red stripe on outside seams. Black leather equipment and boots, brass buckles. Dark grey greatcoat roll. Hide-covered haversack.

33

35

34

cloak of respectability. The Prussians inflicted the decisive defeat upon the Danes at Düppel, thus paving the way for the ultimate annexation of the duchies by—Prussia!

The 1866 war with Austria was more deliberately engineered for the purposes of eliminating Austria from the German scene politically, as it now was economically. As a preliminary, those states which made an appearance of supporting Austria and lay near to hand—Hanover, Hesse-Cassel and Saxony—were overrun. Six weeks later, the Austrians went down before the Prussians at the battle of Sadowa, and to the surprise of all (including the Prussians themselves) Germany had new masters. For the moment, however, only Hanover, Hesse-Cassel, Nassau and Frankfurt were annexed outright.

The consequences to the French of their bid to retain the primacy of Europe by declaring war on Prussia in 1870 have already been related. For the Prussians the prizes brought home from the campaign by their army were richer than even the most sanguine among them had expected. Bismarck was able to present it as a 'German' crusade, and amid the excitements and alarms of the war, produced the bizarre 'German Empire' —a sham constitution which hid the reality of the Prussian state's possession of the resources of all Germany.

The capital of Europe was Berlin, and the soldiers had made it so at Sedan and Metz.

Under the terms of the Imperial state structure, the individual states' regiments did not lose their identity altogether when they were taken into the Imperial army. Prussian equipment and dress was adopted, but subsidiary titles and state helmet badges proclaimed the state of origin. Local sentiment was still very strong, and strongest of all in Bavaria. A condition of that state's entry into the Empire was a separate existence of the Bavarian army in time of peace, and it was recognisable by the characteristic light blue uniforms (see G33). The units of Saxony (which had joined the Prussian 'North German Confederation' in 1867), and Baden and Wurttemberg (both of which, together with the Bavarians, had fought alongside the Prussians in 1870) were also clearly distinct. In practice, however, there was no possibility of any of them being other than additions to the total strength of the Prussian army.

Imperial Germany, 1871-1918

Swollen by the regiments and manpower of the other German states, the Prussian army was never so splendid as in the years leading up to the First World War, a time when it had no campaigns in Europe and none of the colonial experience of the French—or even the British! (The grey-uniformed Germans in the paltry colonies picked up in Africa offered no excitements. There was a chance in 1900 when the Chinese patriots known as the 'Boxers' attacked the European quarter in Peking and murdered the German minister. A German contingent was sent out to join the international punitive force, and was exhorted from the dockside by Kaiser William II to obtain a reputation like that of 'the Huns a thousand years ago under Attila'. Alas for his hopes, they arrived too late! Others had put down the Boxers.)

The Garde du Corps of Prussia still wore the uniform as G30, and Cuirassiers G28 but with the white breeches and jacked boots of G30 in parade dress. After 1888 the cuirass was worn only on parades. Dragoon regiments wore a uniform as G47, but with a single-breasted tunic piped down the front. (An example of regimental facings—Dragoon Regiment No. 4 had yellow facings and piping, with brass buttons.) Guard Dragoons wore the Guard Star on their helmets and shoulder-belt pouches, and the Guard Lace on their collars and cuffs.

The Lancer uniform is illustrated as G38, and other examples of facing colours are the red of Regiment No. 3 and the yellow of Regiment No. 15. Guard Lancers wore Guard Lace on collars and cuffs (see G1) and the Guard Star on their pouches. Hussars continued to be the most colourful of the cavaliers, especially the Life Hussar Regiments with their death's head badges (see G64) and all-black uniforms, braided and piped white. Both wore white plumes, but the 1st Regiment rode white horses and had red bags on their hussar caps, while the 2nd Regiment rode blacks and had blue bags. They were highly favoured in that the Kaiser was the Colonel-in-Chief of both, his son the Crown Prince commanded the 1st on the eve of the war, and his daughter, Princess Victoria Louise, was a second Colonel-in-Chief to the 2nd.

A similar uniform, all black with white plume (standing erect) and red bag was worn by the Brunswick Hussar Regiment, No. 17. This regiment had been formed in 1809 as part of the Duke of Brunswick's Black Corps, and wore the badge of that formation (see G63). The braiding and piping of this regiment was yellow, and they wore blue and white girdles.

Other variations were the brown tunics of the 4th Hussars, the light blue of the 9th and the dark green of the 11th. There was also a Life Guard Hussar Regiment, which wore an upright white-over-black plume and the Guard Star on its caps (with a red bag) and pouches, yellow braiding and piping, black and white girdle, black fur trim and red-fronted sabretache, but otherwise appeared much as G36.

The standard infantry dress was the small spiked helmet,

dating from 1867, and dark blue single-breasted tunic of the
Prussian army with, normally, the 'Brandenburg' cuff (G42).
Collar, cuffs, button flap, piping down the front and on the
skirts (as G24) were red, but shoulder-straps indicated by their
colour the Army Corps in which the regiment was placed (e.g.
Army Corps X based on Hanover wore white straps, Army
Corps XI based on Cassel wore scarlet), and each contained
seven to eleven regiments. Some regiments, however, wore the
'Swedish' cuff (G23), and Guard regiments wore Guard Lace
on their collars and cuffs (as G44), which included these regiments which held Guard status in their own states but were
numbered in the line of the Imperial army. Dark blue-grey
trousers, striped red, were worn in winter and white in summer.
Only two regiments—1st Foot Guards and 1st Guard Grenadier Regiment—wore on parade the grenadier cap (G31), a
privilege they shared with the Kaiser's bodyguard, the Schloss-
gardekompagnie.

Rifle regiments wore a green tunic with scarlet facings and
piping, 'Swedish' cuffs and a leather shako (G43) but the Guard
Schützen Battalion had black collars and 'French' cuffs (G41),
piped red.

Artillery wore a similar uniform, the distinctives being black
collars and 'Swedish' cuffs for Field Artillery and 'Brandenburg' for Foot Artillery, both piped red, and a ball on the
helmet instead of a spike (G46). Another type of uniform was
that worn by machine-gun units, first formed in 1901. These

G36 3rd Hussars, 1892.
*Trooper. Cap: black fur; red bag; white plume and cap
lines; national cockade (Prussian); white metal title
plate; brass chinstrap. Tunic: red; white braid, piping and
girdle. Dark blue breeches with white stripe on outside
seams. Pelisse: blue; white braid; grey fur. White
shoulder-belt, black pouch. Black leather sword-slings
and sabretache, with royal cypher in yellow. Black boots
with white trimming.*

G37 Rear of Hussar tunic.

G38 16th Lancers, 1892.
*Trooper. Cap: black leather; brass fittings; mid-blue top,
piped white; white cap lines; white plume as G36 when
worn. Tunic: dark blue; mid-blue collar, cuffs, plastron
front and piping; white metal buttons; mid-blue shoulder-
straps with brass crescents. Mid-blue and dark blue
girdle. White belt and sword slings, black pouch. Dark
blue breeches, black boots.*

G39 Rear of Lancer Tunic.

72

36

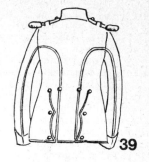

39

38

37

wore a grey-green uniform with scarlet facings and piping and 'Swedish' cuffs, and a grey-green felt shako of the same design as the Rifles. There were two Guard detachments, and the second wore the black facings and 'French' cuff of the Guard Schützen Battalion.

Among the other states it was principally the Saxon and the Bavarian units which exhibited an independent tradition while adopting Prussian equipment and styles. Saxon cavalry units wore light-blue uniforms (compare G34), and their artillery green tunics with red piping, collars, cuffs and piping around the edge of the shoulder-straps. There was a distinctive 'Saxon' cuff and skirt piping (see G46), and also a 'Saxon' shako for their rifle regiments. Bavarian cavalry regiments for the most part wore the dark green associated with them in the past, and their dragoons and infantry wore light blue (compare G19 and G33). Ordinary infantry wore red facings and piping, and rifle regiments green. The reader will remember that it was the Bavarian army which Adolf Hitler, the Austrian, joined on the outbreak of war in 1914.

Throughout the Imperial army, the Prussian tradition of red plumes and 'swallows' nests' for musicians of all arms was

G40 **General Officer, 1892.**
Full dress. Helmet: black leather; brass fittings; white feather plume. Tunic: blue, piped white (rear as G24); gilt buttons; scarlet collar and cuffs; gold lace, shoulder cords and aiguillette. Silver sash, white gloves. Dark blue-grey trousers with double red stripe down outside seams.

G41 'French' cuff.

G42 'Brandenburg' cuff.

G43 **2nd Silesian Jäger Battalion, 1892.**
Musician NCO. Shako: black; brass plate; Prussian national cockade. Tunic: green; scarlet collar, cuffs, shoulder straps, 'swallow's nests', and piping front and rear (G24); gold NCO's lace on collar, cuffs and 'nests'. Dark blue-grey trousers with red stripe down outside seams. Black belt, white gloves and music pouch.

G44 **1st Baden Life Grenadier Regiment, No. 109, 1914.**
Private in marching order. Helmet: black leather; white metal fittings and state griffin badge; brass chinscales. Tunic: blue; scarlet collar, cuffs, piping front and rear (G24); silver Guard lace; white metal buttons; white shoulder-strap with red crown badge. Dark blue-grey trousers, red stripes down outside seams. Black boots and equipment straps. Hide pack, dark grey greatcoat roll, buff haversack on right hip.

40

41

42

43

44

maintained.

In 1910 field-service uniform was introduced into the army of a colour described as 'field-grey'. Worn with natural leather equipment, it preserved the general appearance of the blue uniforms and still included such features as piping, styled cuffs and helmets. Thus Hussars still wore fur caps and full-braided tunics, Lancers plastron-fronts and lance-caps. Rifle regiments even wore a distinctively green shade of 'field-grey'. In other words, it was a more radical reform of uniform than that undertaken in the French army at the time, but not as radical as the khaki and flat caps of the contemporary British army, undifferentiated except for badges and buttons and, of course, kilts and glengarries in Highland regiments. As the German uniform combined service utility with the no less real benefits of the visible reminders of history, they may be said to have arrived at the best solution to the problems of clothing troops for war as it was then practised. If, however, the reader is a thoroughgoing radical himself, he might be inclined to the view that these matters did indicate the relative degrees of conservatism in the three armies. Certainly, their ultimate performance in the field would seem to give support for that

G45 1st Saxon Jäger Battalion, 1892.
> *Rifleman in field marching order. Shako: black hair plume; black cover; (underneath, black with a brass star). Tunic: green; black collar and cuffs; red piping around bottom of collar, tunic front and bottoms, skirts (as for G46), shoulder straps; white metal buttons. Black leather equipment and boots but red rifle strap. Dark blue-grey trousers with red stripe down outside seams. Equipment as G44.*

G46 Saxon Foot Artillery, 1892.
> *Lieutenant in parade dress. Helmet: black leather, brass fittings. Tunic: green; red collar, cuffs, shoulder-strap base, and piping down front, bottom edges and skirts; eight gilt buttons down front; silver shoulder-strap cording and crescents. Silver sash lined with light blue. Red sword slings faced with gold lace. White gloves. Dark blue-grey trousers with red stripe down outside seam. Black boots.*

G47 2nd Wurttemberg Dragoon Regiment, 1892.
> *Dragoon. Helmet: black leather with white metal fittings but brass chinscales. Tunic: mid-blue, yellow collar, shoulder straps, cuffs, piping down front and skirts (as G24); white metal buttons. White belts and sword slings. Dark grey breeches, black boots*

76

45

46

47

opinion, for of the three the French were least prepared, and the British the most, for the tactics of the magazine-rifle armies.

Confident of the superiority of their staffwork, the Germans placed a great reliance upon the Schlieffen Plan—the plan for the opening campaign for a war on two fronts, the German nightmare. It incorporated the Prussian ideal of a swift knock-out blow to be delivered by the bulk of the German army striking west against the French, followed later by an attack on the slower Russian forces in the east. In being by 1905, and exercising a fatal influence on the obstructive conduct of German diplomacy in the crisis which preceded the outbreak of war, it failed in the execution—but only just! Nor could the responsibility for failure be laid upon the German soldiers, who marched and fought to the point of total exhaustion to keep up with the timetable of operations demanded by the Plan.

Not that the army was broken yet; its opponents were as worn by the hard service, and the German army held great tracts of vital French territory from which they would have to be dislodged if victory was to go to the Allies. The German govern-

G48 Lancer Regiment, 1914.
      Lancer in field-service dress. Field-grey throughout, with dark cap cover and natural leather equipment and boots. Piping on tunic as G38 and G39, white, with light blue on collar, shoulder-straps and cuffs (Regiment No. 16); white metal buttons.

G49 42nd Infantry Regiment, (5th Pomeranian), 1914.
      Private in field-service dress. Field-grey throughout, with natural leather equipment and boots. Tunic piping in red (rear as G24), also helmet numeral; brass buttons.

G50 Guard Field Artillery Regiment, No. 1, 1915.
      NCO in full dress. Field-grey throughout. Cap: black band, piped red top and bottom, also top brim; top cockade red, white and black ('Reichscocade'), bottom the black and white Prussian cockade; black leather peak. Tunic: black collar and cuffs, piped red on top, gold NCO's lace and Guard lace; shoulder-straps red piped white, yellow grenade badge, red piping front and rear (G24); brass buttons. Black belt, brass buckle. Red stripe on outside seam of trousers.

G51 Shoulder-strap, 1914 full dress.
      1st Bavarian Life Regiment. Yellow crown on red.

G52 Shoulder-strap, 1914 field-service dress.
      12th (Saxon) Jäger Battalion. Grey-green strap, piped green; red numeral and horn.

G

51

52

48

49

50

ment did not expect that to happen. It had already formulated its war-aim as the creation of 'a central European economic association through customs treaties . . . (which) . . . will not have any common constitutional supreme authority and all its members will be formally equal, but in practice will be under German leadership and must stabilise Germany's economic dominance over Mitteleuropa . . .' The other European states were to be forced into this economic union as and when victory in the field allowed. This is what the First World War was about; the reader may feel it has a familiar sound.

Already there was a feeling of the German peace about, as Allied soldiers were hurled to their deaths on German barbed wire in France. New regulations for full-dress uniforms were issued in September 1915, which relegated the historic dark blue to proud memory, and substituted a field-grey version set off with traditional items such as cuffs and piping (see G50).

At the same time a new field-service dress which moved more in the direction of pure utility was introduced, especially in the new tunic, or 'bluse', of which only the shoulder straps bore distinctives such as coloured piping and numerals. It was worn at first with the 'pickelhaube' with the spike removed or a flat field-service cap until the steel trench helmet was brought into use in the spring of 1916. These changes were made when supplies allowed, and as the allied economic blockade of Germany began to be effective, shortages of all kinds occurred, leading to the disappearance of, say, the marching boot in favour of ankle boots and puttees (see G53).

The rise of Hitler, 1919-40

The German army in the East broke the Russians and by the enforced Treaty of Brest-Litovsk laid the foundations of the expected German economic empire there. The vision was shattered by the final failure of the army in the west. The subsequent recovery of German diplomacy, underwritten by the economic revival and pushed to new lengths by the rise of Hitler to power will be quite familiar to the reader.

By the Treaty of Versailles the German army was reduced to a hundred thousand men, a repetition of similar limitations imposed upon the Prussian army after Jena. The response of the army was the same: to consider the reduced force as a trained nucleus upon which later war-effective forces could be built, evading the restrictions whenever possible by such means as the 1921 agreement with the Communist government of Russia. This set up in Russia jointly managed factories to make shells and poison-gas for both, and tank and flying schools. This co-operation continued until Hitler ended it in 1933. The reduction was even beneficial, in that it dissolved the old state-army loyalties and created a simple loyalty to the national army, now really unified, and rid the army of much material which was or would soon be obsolete.

With the arrival of Hitler, the process of rebuilding the Reichswehr came out into the open. In 1934 all ranks took an oath of unconditional obedience to his person as 'supreme commander of the armed forces'. In the following year, conscription was reintroduced and a dress uniform which was the same for all ranks (G54). The subservience of the army to the Nazi Party's grip on the state was emphasised by the imposition of party insignia (G55, G56, G58) although at this stage the party salute of outstretched arm was not required as it was later.

Following a development initiated in the Regulations of 1915, the various arms of service were distinguished by coloured piping, or Waffenfarbe. The basic system was as follows:

Carmine: general staff, veterinary corps.
Bright red: artillery, generals.
White: infantry.
Gold yellow: cavalry.
Lemon: signals.
Rose pink: armoured troops.
Light green: rifle battalions, mountain troops.
Cornflower blue: medical corps.
Light blue: mechanical supply troops.
Black: engineers.

An important change in 1935 was the issue of a smaller-pattern helmet (compare G53 and G54), which gave the German soldiers of the Second World War a more purposeful appearance than those of the First. Off parade, a peaked field-grey cap with a blue-green band (G59 is an extreme example) decorated according to the wearer's rank, was prescribed.

To complete the events of that memorable year when the German army emerged from the shadows of Versailles, the standards of the old Imperial Guard Regiments were handed over to its custody at a symbolic parade in Berlin. It is an interesting point whether in time a new Guard would have emerged. There was such a move, perhaps, in 1939 when a new uniform was designed for Infantry Regiment Grossdeutschland, with 'French' cuffs as worn by the former Guard Schützen Battalion. War, however, overtook the experiment. In any case, the private Party army, the SS, fulfilled the functions of a Guard. The Schutz Staffel was founded in 1925 as a personal bodyguard for Hitler, and began its expansion four years later as an elite force under the sinister figure of Himmler. After the Nazi accession to power, Himmler linked the secret police forces to it, especially the Gestapo, the Prussian secret police founded in 1933 by Goering. Given the pick of manpower and indoctrinated with racial fanaticism, it was a formidable force, from which sprang the Waffen SS divisions later. It was naturally resented by the regular army, the Reichswehr, and is outside the scheme of this book.

The true elite of the army were the armoured troops, the Panzertruppen. A service uniform, suitable for all normal occasions and field service, was introduced in 1936 (G60) and became the standard wear of the German army thereafter. A special black uniform was provided for the Panzer troops, however, which was in part functional but also marked them as a breed apart, favoured ones (see G61 and G67). Each of the leading armies at this time had its small group of tank visionaries: in Germany it was led by Major Guderian, who found a powerful backer in Hitler. The first German tank battalion was established in 1934; three divisions with 561 tanks came into being the following year. On the outbreak of war German tank strength stood at over 3,100. The tank doctrine had been preached more effectively in Germany than elsewhere because it held out the promise of the quick 'knock-out' in the opening campaign which had been the Prussian ideal since the days of

G53 Field service uniform, 1917.
   Tunic and trousers, field-grey. Piping of the shoulder-straps in the colour of the arm of service (e.g. green for Light Infantry). Helmet, basically olive drab. Equipment as for G49.

G54 Dress uniform, 1936.
   Helmet: field-grey, black leather strap, badges G57 on right, G58 on left. Tunic: field-grey, collar, shoulder-straps and cuffs dark blue-green; piping on tunic front and rear (in the style of G24), edges of collar, cuffs and straps in the colour of the arm of the service (e.g. infantry —white); silver braid on collar and cuffs. Trousers: plain grey, piped as above. Black leather equipment and boots.

G55 National emblem.
   Worn on tunic right breast, silver backed by dark blue-green.

G56 Belt buckle.
   White metal.

G57 Helmet badge.
   National colours, black, white and red.

G58 Helmet badge.
   Silver on black.

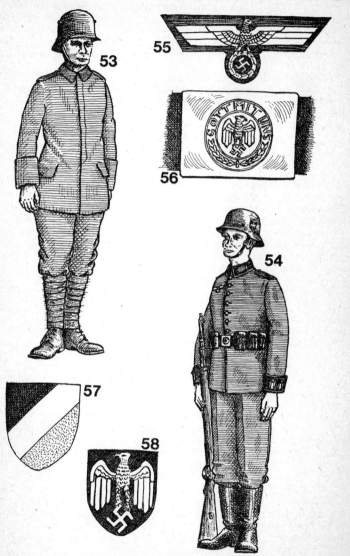

53

55

56

54

57

58

Frederick the Great. Battle experience was to expose weaknesses in German tank design and tactical employment, but they were still well ahead of everyone else. The crewmen, however, were a picked elite and made aware of it: true professional soldiers. In 1939 and 1940 they shattered Europe into pieces.

The illustrations G62-G67 are intended to show the survival of certain items of regimental tradition. The death's head badge of the Duke of Brunswick's Black Corps passed to Brunswick Infantry Regiment No. 92 and the Brunswick Hussar Regiment No. 17. After the First World War, the traditions of these regiments passed to the 1st and 4th Companies of the 17th Infantry Regiment and 4th Squadron of the 13th Mounted Regiment. The other death's head of the old 1st and 2nd Life Hussars passed to the 1st and 2nd Squadrons of the 5th Mounted Regiment. Yet another badge (not illustrated) was the heraldic eagle of the 1st Brandenburg Dragoon Regiment, which was passed on to the 2nd and 4th Squadrons of the 6th Mounted Regiment in 1921. These badges in due course were worn on the caps of expanded formations built up upon the cadres which had maintained the continuity between the old army and the new.

The manner in which Hitler restored the great German Reich and brought within its fold the Germans of the old Austrian empire is well known, and this phase reached its climax with

G59 General, 1940.
   Cap: field-grey top; dark blue-green band; black leather peak; gold cords and piping; silver insignia. Tunic: field-grey; dark blue-green collar with red patches and gold insignia; red shoulder-strap with gold and silver cords; gilt buttons. Breeches: grey with a double red stripe down outside seams. Belt, boots and gloves, brown.

G60 Senior NCO, 1940.
   Service dress. Field service cap: field-grey; cloth national emblem and cockade on front, plus an inverted chevron in the arm of service colour (e.g. infantry—white). Tunic: field-grey; collar and shoulder-straps dark blue-grey; silver braid edging and rank insignia; field-grey buttons. Field-grey trousers, black leather belt and boots.

G61 Tank troops, 1940.
   Black beret, tunic and trousers worn by all ranks. Piping on edge of collar, collar patches and shoulder-straps, rose pink (but 24 Panzer Division used the cavalry yellow, being originally 1st Cavalry Division). Mouse-grey shirt, black tie. Black leather belt and boots.

G

59

60

61

THE RISE OF HITLER

the army's lightning campaign in Poland in September 1939. Over fifty German divisions were now available, including six of Panzers, and supported by 1,600 aircraft—a total of one and a half million ground troops. The whole operation was covered by a diplomatic agreement with the only force which might have prevented it, the communist government of Russia. The episode opened up new vistas of power, and revived dreams of the unachieved aims of 1914. By the summer of the following year, a series of equally quick victories in the west had created subject German provinces out of France, the Low Countries and Denmark and Norway, and the soldiers were faced about to the east. After preliminary campaigns to subdue the Balkans, on 22nd June 1941 the German army was launched into Russia.

G62 Brunswick 'Leib-Battalion', 1815.
   Private. Uniform black throughout. Light-blue collar, shoulder-straps and trouser stripes. White metal badge.

G63 'Death's head' badge, 1939.
   Worn by designated portions of 17th Infantry Regiment and 13th Cavalry Regiment.

G64 'Death's head' badge of the Life Hussar Regiments, 1914.

G65 Shoulder-strap, squadron sergeant-major, 5th Cavalry Regiment, 1939.
   Dark blue-green strap, silver braid and badges, yellow piping on edge.

G66 'Death's head' badge.
   Worn between the national cockade and national emblem on the caps of designated squadrons of the 5th Cavalry Regiment, 1939.

G67 Collar patch, 1939.
   White 'death's head'. Black patch for all tank troops, with rose pink piping for all but 24th Panzer Division (yellow).

62

63

64

65

66

67

BIBLIOGRAPHY

There is an embarrassing wealth of material for two phases of this subject—the French army in the time of Napoleon, and the German army of the Second World War.

For the first, the two volumes of *The Uniforms and Equipment of the Soldiers of the First Empire* by Liliane and Fred Funcken, published by Casterman, 1969, are basic. Readers who have no French should not be deterred; it is easy to follow the captions and tabulated information from the good illustrations. The work deals also with the other armies involved in the wars, and therefore with German soldiers.

There is nothing comparable for any other period. *French Army Regiments and Uniforms* by W. A. Thorburn, published by Arms and Armour Press, 1969, has an excellent text which takes the development of the French army to 1871. It is accompanied by good black-and-white prints.

David Nash's well illustrated books for Almark Publications are indispensable. At the time of writing, they comprise *The Prussian Army, 1808–1815* (1972), *German Artillery, 1914–1918* (1971 reprinted), and *German Infantry, 1914–1918* (1971). The same publisher promises works on German cavalry of the First World War.

For the German army of the Second World War, *German Army Uniforms and Insignia 1933–1945* by Brian Davis, Arms and Armour Press, second edition 1973, has established itself as the standard work on the subject which will not quickly be superseded.

Issues of *Tradition* magazine, published by Belmont-Maitland, yield information which 'plugs the gaps', but it is not systematic enough for most reference purposes.

Until wargamers and modellers can be wooed away from Waterloo and 'Operation Barbarossa' there is little hope of an improvement.

INDEX OF FRENCH ARMY

INDEX OF GERMAN ARMY

Some titles available in the 'Discovering' series

American Story in England (25p)
Antique Firearms (25p)
Archaeology in Denmark (40p)
Archaeology in England and Wales (40p)
Artillery (30p)
Banknotes (30p)
Bath Road (25p)
Berkshire (20p)
Bird Watching (30p)
Birmingham Road (25p)
Brasses and Brassrubbing (30p)
British Cavalry Regiments (30p)
British Military Uniforms (30p)
British Postage Stamps (30p)
Castle Combe (15p)
Caves (30p)
Chesham (30p)
Christian Names (30p)
Christmas Customs and Folklore (30p)
Churches (35p)
Civic Heraldry (25p)
Comics (30p)
Derbyshire/Peak District (30p)
Devon (20p)
Dorset (30p)
Ecology (30p)
Edged Weapons (30p)
English Civil Wargaming (30p)
English County Regiments (25p)
English Customs and Traditions (30p)
English Furniture 1500-1720 (25p)
English Furniture 1720-1830 (30p)
Epitaphs (30p)
Essex (30p)
Exeter Road (25p)
Famous Battles: Marlborough's
 Campaigns (30p)
Famous Battles: Peninsular War (30p)
Folklore of Birds and Beasts (35p)
Footsteps through London's Past (30p)
Forests of Central England (30p)
Gardening for the Handicapped (30p)
Ghosts (30p)
Gloucester Road (25p)
Harness and Saddlery (30p)
Herbs (30p)
Highwaymen (25p)
Hill Figures (35p)
Investing Your Money (30p)
Kings and Queens (35p)

Leicestershire/Rutland (30p)
Life-boats (30p)
Local History (30p)
London for Children (30p)
London – Statues and Monuments (25p)
Mermaids and Sea Monsters (20p)
Militaria (30p)
Military Traditions (30p)
Modelling for Wargamers (30p)
Model Soldiers (30p)
Narrow Gauge Railways (30p)
Norfolk (20p)
Off-beat Walks in London (30p)
Oil Lamps (30p)
Old Buses and Trolleybuses (30p)
Old Motorcycles (30p)
Period Gardens (30p)
Playing-Cards and Tarots (30p)
Railwayana (30p)
Rules for Wargaming (40p)
Schools (35p)
Sea Shells (30p)
Ship Models (30p)
Somerset (30p)
Space (30p)
Spas (30p)
Staffordshire (30p)
Staffordshire Figures (30p)
Stained Glass (35p)
Stately Homes (30p)
Statues in C. and N. England (25p)
Statues in S. England (30p)
Suffolk (25p)
Surnames (30p)
Sussex (30p)
This Old House (35p)
Towns (35p)
Trade Tokens (30p)
Victorian and Edwardian Furniture (35p)
Walks in the Chilterns (35p)
Wargames (35p)
The Westward Stage (45p)
Wild Plant Names (30p)
Wiltshire (30p)
Windsor (25p)
Worcestershire/Herefordshire (30p)
Wrought Iron (25p)
Yorkshire – West Riding (30p)
Your Family Tree (35p)

Printed in England by Maund & Irvine Ltd., Tring, Herts.